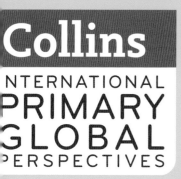

Collins
INTERNATIONAL PRIMARY GLOBAL PERSPECTIVES

T0340446

Student's Book 5

William Collins' dream of knowledge for all began with the publication of his first book in 1819.

A self-educated mill worker, he not only enriched millions of lives, but also founded a flourishing publishing house. Today, staying true to this spirit, Collins books are packed with inspiration, innovation and practical expertise.

They place you at the centre of a world of possibility and give you exactly what you need to explore it.

Collins. Freedom to teach.

Published by Collins

An imprint of HarperCollins*Publishers*
The News Building, 1 London Bridge Street, London,
SE1 9GF, UK

HarperCollins*Publishers*
Macken House, 39/40 Mayor Street Upper, Dublin 1, D01 C9W8

Browse the complete Collins catalogue at
collins.co.uk

British Library Cataloguing-in-Publication Data

A catalogue record for this publication is available from the British Library.

Series editor: Nick Coates
Author: Katharine Meunier
Publisher: Elaine Higgleton
Product developer: Roisin Leahy
Development editor: Sonya Newland
Copyeditor: Catherine Dakin
Proofreader: Gudrun Kaiser
Text permissions researcher: Rachel Thorne
Cover designer: Gordon MacGilp
Typesetter: David Jimenez, Ken Vail Graphic Design
Production controller: Lyndsey Rogers
Printed in India by Multivista Global Pvt. Ltd.

We are grateful to MInal Mistry for providing feedback on the Student's Book as it was developed.

Contents

How to use this book

Use this book in your lessons, to learn about a range of global topics!

The skills box shows you the main and subsidiary skills that you will learn and practise in this lesson.

Key terms

Key terms are important words or phrases that will help you to understand what to do in each lesson.

Vocabulary

The definitions provided will help you to understand words in reading texts.

Useful language

The useful phrases and sentences provided will help you to discuss the topic …

- An activity that involves reading
- An activity that involves writing
- An activity that involves speaking
- An activity where you work independently
- An activity that involves working in a pair
- An activity that involves working in a group

Talking point

You will look back on what you have learned in the lesson, and talk about things that went well with your classmates.

Before you go

- Think about how you will use your new skills!

Unit 1 Emergency! Emergency!

What do you know?
- What do the emergency services do?
- How can we prevent an emergency?
- What can we do to help people who are in trouble?
- What helps us to predict disasters caused by nature?

In this unit, you will:
- use communication to share important information
- create infographics to explain and inform
- write questions to help you to search emergency response systems
- work in teams to solve problems
- research difficult environments to make survival plans.

1.1 Don't panic

✓ Collaboration
✓ Communication

1 👥 💬 **What is an emergency? Discuss your ideas.**

2 👥 💬 **What emergency events have happened to you or someone in your family?
Play 'Find someone who has …'.
Use the worksheet.**

Have you ever got lost?

3 📖 **Read and respond.**

ICAO spelling alphabet						
A Alfa	**B** Bravo	**C** Charlie	**D** Delta	**E** Echo	**F** Foxtrot	**G** Golf
H Hotel	**I** India	**J** Juliett	**K** Kilo	**L** Lima	**M** Mike	**N** November
O Oscar	**P** Papa	**Q** Quebec	**R** Romeo	**S** Sierra	**M** Tango	**U** Uniform
V Victor	**W** Whiskey	**X** X-ray	**Y** Yankee	**Z** Zulu		

A spelling alphabet is a set of words that stand for letters of an alphabet when spoken. The chart shows the words used by pilots when communicating with each other. In the early 20th century, people began to use radios to send important messages. Letters like M and N or F and S sound very similar over the radio. This alphabet helped them to avoid misunderstandings. The words in the spelling alphabet were chosen because they sound different from each other. The ICAO tested these words on 31 different nationalities to make sure that the alphabet could be understood. This version of the International Civil **Aviation** Organisation's (ICAO) spelling alphabet has been used since 1956. It still helps pilots, **air traffic controllers** and other professionals all over the world to understand one another.

a Answer the questions.

- Who uses this alphabet?
- Why do they use it?
- How do they use it?
- How does it help different nationalities to communicate with each other?

b Spell your name to a partner using the alphabet.

4 Read the instructions for the game 'Line of communication'. Decide how you will work as a team. Play the game.

Line of communication game

You will need:

- a copy of the ICAO spelling alphabet
- scrap paper for writing short messages.

Instructions:

1 In teams, agree what order you will take in the line of communication.
2 Space yourselves out so that other teams will not hear you.
3 The first team member collects a message. They relay the message to the next team member using the spelling alphabet.
4 The second team member passes the message along to the third team member.
5 Continue until the message reaches the last member of the team.
6 The last team member completes the task in the message.

Talking point

Did you work well as a team today? What did you do to make it a success?

Before you go

What do you need to think about when you communicate? Choose one word. Put all your words together to create and display a class word cloud about communication.

1.2 Natural disasters

✓ Collaboration
✓ Communication

1 👥 📖 💬 **Find out about natural hazards.
Read the statement. Do you agree?**

> If a hurricane hits land where no one lives, it isn't a disaster; it's weather.
> A disaster is when a natural hazard meets a human population.

2 👥 ✏️ **Look at the picture. List three ways that the building design helps to protect people from a flood.**

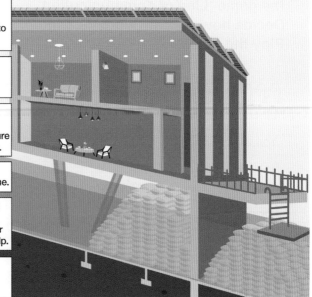

Emergency water is collected when water runs down the roof into a large storing barrel.

Solar panels on roof give power if there is a local power cut.

Roof and floors have insulation. This helps to keep the temperature in the home the same.

Sandbags stop water from entering the home.

Platform allows direct access for a boat. This could be used for supplies or rescue help.

The home is raised 2 metres above ground level.

3 📖 **Read the information opposite, about how engineers collaborate.**

  a 👥 💬 How do engineers work together?

  b 👥 💬 Which design do you like best? Why?

4 📖 **Read and respond.**

> **Engineers needed!**
> Team task: Build a shelter that can withstand a strong wind.
> You will need: 6 pieces of card
> Time: 5 minutes

  a 👤 ✏️ Draw your own idea of the structure.

  b 👥 💬 Share your designs. Decide on a final design and then build it.

  c 👥 💬 ✏️ Test your structures. Record your results.

Talking point

How well do you think you worked as a team today? What did you do to make the challenge a success? How could you improve next time?

Before you go

Why is it useful for engineers around the world to collaborate with one another?

Engineers collaborate!

Engineers around the world **collaborate**, sharing their skills, knowledge and understanding. They look at scientific research into the causes and behaviour of Earth's natural forces. They use this information to help people survive natural disasters by designing buildings that help to reduce, remove or **predict** the effects of natural **hazards**. Engineers need good problem-solving skills! They experiment with different designs, methods and materials.

Fire-resistant home

The design of this home is based on a fallen log. The building is covered with **corrugated** iron. This material is **flexible** and strong and it will not burn. Its curved shape also stops leaves and branches from collecting on the roof. This is very important in places where forest fires happen.

Indestructible concrete beach house

This beach house was designed to protect it against hurricanes. It is made of a special type of extra-strong **concrete**. Its flat roof cannot be lifted by winds. The house is also built on a raised platform to help protect it against flooding.

Flood-proof house

This home is in a flood zone. **Stilts** are designed to lift it 2 metres above the river bank and higher than flood level. The house has a light metal frame. Water can flow beneath it. People can enter by boat, onto a metal staircase.

Vocabulary

hazards: unavoidable risks or dangers

corrugated: having rows of folds that look a bit like waves

flexible: able to be bent easily without breaking

indestructible: something that is very strong and cannot be destroyed

concrete: a strong building material made of broken stones, sand and cement

stilts: long, thin poles that keep something off the ground

Key terms

collaborate: when two or more people work together on a task

predict: to think what will happen in the future

1.3 Imaging weather

✓ Research
✓ Reflection

1 **What do you know about weather?**

a 👥 💬 Describe the weather outside the window.

b 👥 💬 What is the weather like in these places?

c How could you find out what the weather is like in different places today?

2 **Look at this weather report.**

a 👥 💬 Use the information to describe the weather.

b 👥 💬 What questions do people ask about the weather and why?

c 👥 💬 **Research question**s help you to find information about a topic or issue. What might a science **researcher** want to find out about the weather?

3 📖 **Read and respond.**

All about satellites

A satellite moves around, or **orbits**, objects in space. The Moon is a natural satellite, because it moves around Earth. Some satellites are artificial, which means they are made by humans. The first artificial satellite was called Sputnik 1. It was **launched** on 4 October 1957. Artificial satellites provide images for maps. They are also used for communication and can help to predict weather.

Weather satellites are taken into orbit by rockets. They are called 'polar orbiting satellites' because they move from north to south over the poles. They circle the planet twice a day at low orbit (800 kilometres above Earth). They provide information about the daily weather.

Other satellites, much further from Earth, are called geostationary satellites. They move at the same speed as Earth. These satellites can predict weather conditions that change over time, such as storms. Not all countries have weather satellites. Countries that do have them share their information with the countries that don't. These satellites help experts to prepare for natural disasters.

Key terms

research questions: the main questions you use to find information during research on a topic

researcher: someone who collects, organises, analyses and interprets data and opinions to explore issues, solve problems and predict

Vocabulary

orbits: moves in a curved path around an object in space

launched: started or set something in motion

a 👥 💬 What questions might the writer have researched to find this information about satellites?

b 📖 👤 ✏️ How are satellites used? Write an explanation.

4 📖 **Read and respond.**

My questions are in a muddle! Can you help me?

a 👥 📖 Match each question with the correct answer.

How do some satellites help mapmakers?	They move at the same speed as Earth.
What is a satellite?	They move from north to south over the poles.
Why do we have weather satellites?	Some satellites provide photos for maps.
Where do polar orbiting satellites go?	It moves around objects in space.
How fast do geostationary satellites move?	They help people to predict temperatures and storms.

b 👥 ✏️ Look at the answers on the worksheet. Write questions to match.

5 **Engineers build homes that can adapt to changes in the climate. To do this, they carry out research to make sure they understand the issue.**

a 👥 ✏️ Fill in the table on the worksheet.

b 👥 ✏️ Use the information to write a research question.

How do you build a home for very hot climates?

Talking point

How good are you at writing questions? Choose bronze, silver or gold.

Before you go

How do satellites help people prepare for natural disasters?

1.4 Emergency response

✓ **Research**
✓ Collaboration

1 **Look at the picture. Then complete the tasks.**

a 👥 💬 Describe what is happening in the picture.

b 👥 ✏️ What else would you like to know? Write a question.

2 📖 **Read the notes by a reporter who interviewed one of the rescue workers. Then answer the questions.**

> Call received at 10 a.m. on 4 June at mountain rescue centre.
>
> Wife of hurt man called by mobile phone.
>
> Accident on side of mountain by a lake.
>
> Man about 40 years old hurt leg – not able to walk.
>
> 2 hours to reach him on foot.
>
> Called ahead to helicopter on radio.
>
> Bad weather – snowing.
>
> Man taken to hospital by helicopter.
>
> Leg broken.

a 👥 💬 What questions do you think the reporter asked to get this information?

b 👥 ✏️ What else would you like to know? Write two more questions.

3 📖 **Read and respond.**

Fact file: Médecins Sans Frontières (MSF)

Médecins Sans Frontières means 'Doctors without Borders'.
It is an international charity. It provides medical help to
people who are affected by war, illness and natural disasters.
Nearly 65 000 people work for MSF, many of them doctors.
The charity was started in 1971 in Paris by a group of journalists and doctors. Now it
works in more than 70 countries and it raises $1.9 billion every year to fund its activities.
It provides nearly 400 000 families a year with packs of food, clothes and bedding to
help in emergency situations. It gives nearly 10 million people every year medical help.

a 🔖 ✏️ Write a question that can be answered from this fact file.

b 🔖 ✏️ Change your question into an interview question.

4 📖 **Imagine you are a team of news reporters. Role-play an interview with someone who works for MSF. Read the example, then follow the steps.**

a 🔖 ✏️ In your groups, write interview questions that would provide answers for all the information in the report.

> What makes your charity international?

> We work in over 70 countries.

b 🔖 💬 Organise your team and carry out your interview. One team member should play the person who works for MSF. The rest of the team should play news researchers.

5 Imagine that your newspaper wants you to find out what local medical charities do in your area. Complete the tasks.

a 🔖 ✏️ Fill in the table on the worksheet. Write a research question. Use the Checklist to make sure your research question works well.

b 🔖 💬 Share and compare. How good are your questions?

Checklist

Research question checklist

✓ Is your question clear and concise?

✓ Is it possible to find this information from sources?

✓ Have you narrowed down the issue to make sure it is focused?

✓ Have you used adjectives to make the question specific?

✓ Will this question help you to find the information you need?

Talking point

How good were you at writing questions today? Do you think you have improved?

Before you go

What skills do you think you need to be a rescue worker?

1.5 **Different views**

1 👥 💬 **How has the man changed his perspective?**

> **Key term**
>
> **perspective:** a viewpoint on an issue based on evidence and reasoning

2 👥 💬 **Sit back to back with a partner. Take turns to describe what you can see. Use the word 'perspective' to compare your viewpoints.**

3 📖 **We often 'see' things differently from someone else. Read the text about Jamal on the worksheet. Then complete the tasks.**

a 👥 💬 Look at the situations below.
How would you feel about each one?
How would your partner feel if these things happened to them? How do you think Jamal would feel?

* Situation 1: Your family gets a cat as a pet.

* Situation 2: You are at a friend's house for dinner and their mum cooks a beef stew.

* Situation 3: You swim in water with fish around you.

* Situation 4: You are going to the doctor for medicine.

You	Your partner	Jamal
I feel … because …	They feel … because …	Jamal might feel … because …

b 👥 💬 In groups, talk about whether your perspectives are the same as or different from Jamal's. Why do you think that is?

4 📖 **Read the text about charities on the worksheet. Then complete the tasks below.**

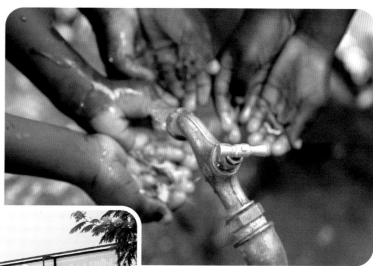

a 🗣️ Find one reason that people support local charities. Find one reason that people support international charities.

b ✏️ Copy and complete the table.

Reasons for choosing local charities	Reasons for choosing international charities
Solve local problems	Help people around the world

c ✏️ Use the notes in your table to write a summary analysing the different perspectives.

Useful language

Some people may disagree with this idea …

Some people may say that … however …

They claim that … since …

However …

But …

On the other hand …

Talking point

How good are you at finding different perspectives?

Before you go

Do *you* think it is better to support local or international charities? Give your reasons.

1.6 Be prepared!

1 What does 'being prepared' mean to you?
Make a list of all the things you need to think about
before you come to school each day.

2 Read and respond.

> **Hope for the best, but prepare for the worst**
>
> One fine day, a fox was out walking in a forest, looking for food. As the
> fox approached a clearing, it saw a wolf sharpening its claws against
> the trunk of a tree. The fox looked about carefully. It couldn't understand
> why the wolf would feel in danger.
>
> The fox went up to the wolf and asked, 'The hunters are not out today,
> nor can I see any other danger, so why are you sharpening your claws?'
>
> The wolf replied, 'Fox! We live in a forest. There are enemies
> everywhere. Who knows when I'll have to use my sharp claws against
> them? If I don't sharpen them now, I may not have time to do so when
> I need them the most.'

a What is the message in
this story?

b Make a list of ways in which
animals prepare themselves for
different situations in the wild.
Use the pictures for ideas.

3 Read and respond.

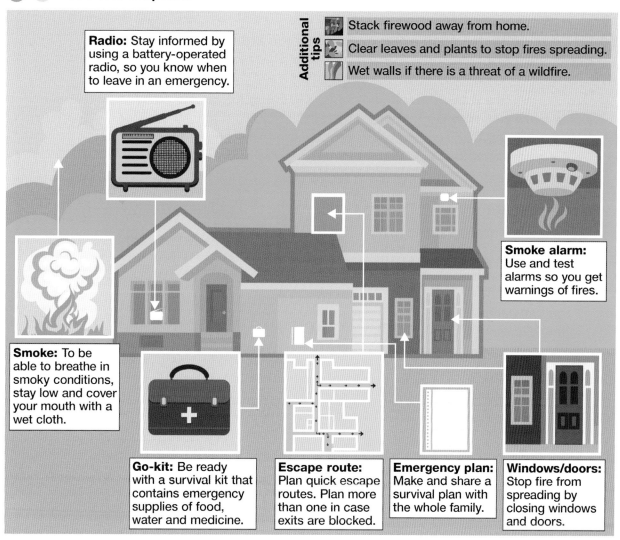

Radio: Stay informed by using a battery-operated radio, so you know when to leave in an emergency.

Additional tips
Stack firewood away from home.
Clear leaves and plants to stop fires spreading.
Wet walls if there is a threat of a wildfire.

Smoke alarm: Use and test alarms so you get warnings of fires.

Smoke: To be able to breathe in smoky conditions, stay low and cover your mouth with a wet cloth.

Go-kit: Be ready with a survival kit that contains emergency supplies of food, water and medicine.

Escape route: Plan quick escape routes. Plan more than one in case exits are blocked.

Emergency plan: Make and share a survival plan with the whole family.

Windows/doors: Stop fire from spreading by closing windows and doors.

a Explain the symbol of the radio. Use the text in the box above it to help you.

b Make a list of things you need to prepare for a wildfire.

4 Conduct a survey to find out how your school prepares for emergencies.

a Look around your school. What signs or objects can you find that would help you in an emergency? Use the worksheet to record your findings.

b What did you find out? Explain how your school prepares for emergencies.

Close the windows → to stop fire spreading

Talking point

How clearly did you explain your reasons for how the school prepares for emergencies?

Before you go

How should we behave in an emergency?

1.7 What causes an earthquake?

✓ Communication
✓ Research

1 👥 💬 In pairs, tell each other everything you know about earthquakes.

> An earthquake is the sudden shaking of the ground. It is caused by the movement of seismic waves through the Earth's rock. They are a natural way for the Earth to release stress. They can cause huge damage to life and property.

2 📖 **Study the diagram about earthquakes in action.**

a 👥 💬 How are numbers and arrows used in this diagram?

b 👥 💬 Use the diagram to explain to your partner how earthquakes happen.

Earthquake in action

1. The sudden unsticking of two tectonic plates releases a massive amount of energy. This causes seismic waves.
2. The waves travel through the Earth and reach its surface.
3. The surface of the Earth cracks or rolls and any buildings start to shake. The shaking can last for several minutes.
4. If the ground is soft, the shaking makes it act like jelly. Buildings sink into the ground.
5. Earthquakes that happen under the sea cause giant waves called tsunamis.

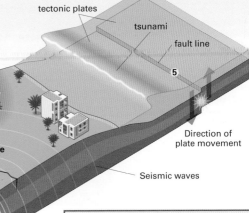

tectonic plates
tsunami
fault line
5
direction of plate movement
tectonic plates
fault line
4
epicentre
Direction of plate movement
Seismic waves
3
2
1
focus

3 📖 👤 ✏️ **Read the text about Measuring earthquakes. How do the diagram and the labelled picture on the next page support the text and help readers to understand the process? Copy the text in the blue box on page 15 and fill in the blanks to explain your ideas.**

Measuring earthquakes

The **Richter scale** has been used since the 1930s to describe the size of an earthquake. The scale measures from zero to ten. An instrument called a **seismograph** is used to **measure earthquakes**. The earthquake shakes the seismograph, and a pen makes marks on a long roll of paper. Scientists study these patterns and use this information to set up early warning systems that help to save lives all over the world. More global research is needed to improve our understanding of earthquakes.

Richter scale

10	Superquake! May happen once every 1000 years
9	Total destruction of large areas
8	Causes death and major **destruction** of whole cities
7	Widespread, serious damage – can be detected all over the world
6	Great damage around the epicentre
5	Furniture moves and poorly-built buildings are damaged
4	People feel shaking and there is some damage close to the epicentre
3	People near the earthquake's epicentre feel this quake
2	Some people may feel the ground shake slightly
0–1	Small quakes, which we can't feel

Measuring earthquakes

A short line that doesn't wiggle very much shows a small earthquake.

A long, very jagged line shows a large earthquake.

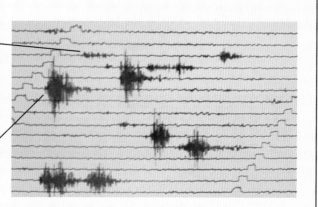

The picture of the seismograph shows … This helps me to understand because …

The way the Richter scale is shown helps me to understand … It shows me …

4 Look at the list of emergency supplies for people who live in earthquake zones. Create an infographic to present this information clearly. Use the Infographic checklist to help you.

fire extinguisher

water supply

medicine

first aid kit

torch and batteries

portable radio and batteries

water and purification tablets

canned and packaged food

camp stove

Checklist

Infographic checklist

✓ Use pictures to support the text.

✓ Give clear, simple information.

✓ Organise the information using headings and/or numbers.

Talking point

How successful was your infographic? Discuss your responses to these questions.

- Did you use pictures to support the text?
- Was your information well-organised, clear and simple?
- What are you most pleased with?
- What will you do to improve next time?

Before you go

What new things have you learned today? Write down three things you have learned from today's lesson.

1.8 **Keep it clear!**

1 👥 💬 **Where might you see these signs?**

2 👥 💬 **Explain the features of this life jacket. How can each feature help in an emergency?**

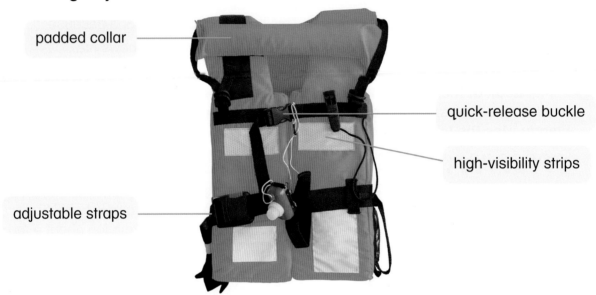

padded collar

quick-release buckle

high-visibility strips

adjustable straps

3 **Prepare a safety demonstration.**

a 👥 💬 Imagine that you are a safety officer on board a boat. In pairs, take turns to explain clearly how to use the life jacket shown above. Your partner should give you feedback based on the Spoken instructions checklist.

b 👥 💬 Present your safety demonstrations. Give each other feedback using the checklist.

c 👥 ✏️ Change the Spoken instructions checklist to make it work for written instructions.

Checklist

Spoken instructions checklist
- ✓ Keep instructions simple.
- ✓ Make sure your voice can be heard clearly.
- ✓ Keep eye contact with the audience.
- ✓ Use gestures to support your words.
- ✓ Use your voice to keep your audience interested.
- ✓ Do not use a script.

4 Look at the images from a safety leaflet on a plane.

a 👥 💬 Match the images to the instructions.

A — Fasten your seat belt like this.

B — Place the mask over your mouth.

C — Exit in the centre of the plane.

b 👥 💬 Why is it important to use pictures for safety instructions on a plane?

c 👥 💬 How are the safety instructions written? Do they match the checklist?

d 👥 💬 Compare the checklist to the one you created in Activity 3c. What is the same? What is different?

5 Look at the emergency instructions on the worksheet.

a 👥 💬 Explain what each picture on the emergency instructions shows.

b 👥 ✏️ Complete the table on the worksheet. Write emergency instructions to show how to **evacuate** a plane on water.

c 👥 💬 Present your emergency instructions to the class. Use the Written instructions checklist to rate each other. How successful were you?

Checklist

Written instructions checklist

✓ Use short, clear instructions.

✓ Use imperative verbs (for example, *place …*, *sit …*).

✓ Use numbers or letters to show the order in which something should be done.

✓ Use diagrams or pictures.

Key term

evacuate: to send someone away from a dangerous place to somewhere safe

Talking point

How good were you at giving instructions? What do you need to do to improve?

Before you go

How could you communicate with someone who does not speak your language?

Unit 1 Final task: Create a survival plan

✓ **Research**
✓ Communication
✓ Reflection

Read the final task and discuss the question.

Work in **teams** to create a **survival plan** for a **difficult environment**. **Produce an infographic** that will help **children aged 8–10** survive in **a jungle, mountain or desert**. The infographic should include a **list of what to take** and **information about food and shelter**. You should **use evidence from research** to support your ideas in the final infographic.

Survival kit

1 👥 💬 **What do you need to do to be successful in the task? Use the words in bold to help you.**

2 **In teams, discuss these difficult environments.**

a 👥 💬 Say what you know about the three environments.

b 👥 💬 Choose one of the places. Share what you already know about your chosen environment.

c 👥 💬 Make a list of things you would need to survive there. Use the questions to help.

- What would you eat? Where would you find food?
- How would you sleep? How would you find or make a shelter?
- How would you move about?
- What dangers would there be? How would you protect yourself?

3 Organise your research.

a   👥 ✏️   What else do you need to know to complete the task? What is your research question?

b   👥 💬   Decide who will research what.

The Environment	Food	Travel	Shelter	Weather

4 👥 ✏️ Do your research. Use the information on the worksheet to help you. Copy and complete the ideas map to make notes about your areas of research.

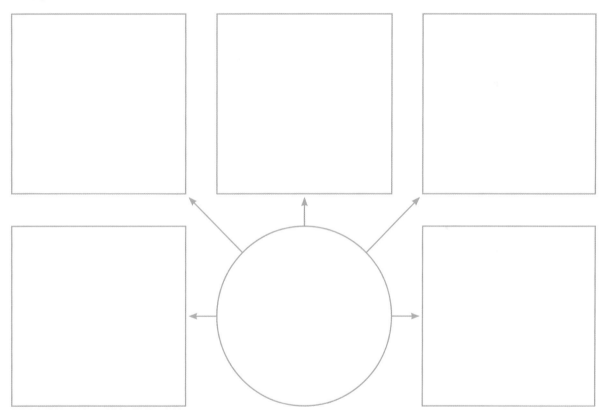

5 👥 ✏️ Use your research to prepare the infographic.

a   In your teams, share your research. Collect all your ideas together to show all your research. Copy and complete a research map like the ideas map in Activity 4.

b   Prepare your infographic. Remember who the presentation is for.

•   Use previous lessons in the unit as a model for your infographic.

•   Use pictures for interest and to add information.

6 👥 💬 Share your survival plan with your audience.

Reflection: How successful was our survival plan?

a   Complete the final task checklist. Use the worksheet.

b   Share your checklist with your team. Do you all agree?

Final task checklist			
Our infographic is clear, simple and easy for children to read.	☺	😐	☹
We used evidence from research that shows an understanding of the difficult environment.	☺	😐	☹
We included information about what to take, food and shelter.	☺	😐	☹
We found information to support our understanding of our chosen environment.	☺	😐	☹
We worked well together as a team.	☺	😐	☹

c   Take turns to say what you did to help the team. Do you all agree?

d   Reflect on your personal perspective. Answer the questions on the worksheet.

Before you go

Discuss these questions in pairs.

What did you enjoy most about this task?

What did you find most difficult about this task?

Did you know how to find the information you needed?

Did you need any help during the task? If yes, who did you ask?

How did you help make the task successful?

How pleased were you with the final infographic?

What would you do differently next time?

Unit 2 Let's communicate!

What do you know?
- What does it mean to have a voice?
- Who listens to you?

In this unit, you will:
- talk about different ways we communicate ideas
- record information using different methods
- research and discuss positive actions for change
- comment on how new information influences opinions.

2.1 Find your voice

1 👥 💬 **Describe this picture using only the names of shapes and their position in relation to each other.**

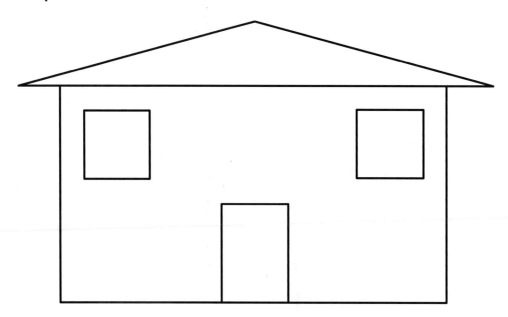

2 👥 💬 **Look at the worksheet. Describe one of the pictures to your partner. Draw the picture your partner describes.**

Draw a large circle.

3 📖 **Read and respond.**

If you want to communicate well, it is important to keep information **short** and **clear**. You should also **present your ideas logically** in steps. Only share **information** that you think is **important and relevant**. **Be polite** to each other. **Listen carefully** and try **not to interrupt** one another.

Key terms

relevant: important or significant to a particular situation or person

a    Explain good communication to your partner in your own words.

b   Use the advice to write a checklist of tips for good communication.

Keep information short and clear.

4 Use your communication skills. Complete the tasks.

a   These children need to line up alphabetically, using their family names. What advice would you give them to help them communicate effectively?

b   Now organise your own group alphabetically.

c   Organise yourselves in the way your teacher tells you.

d   How effectively did you communicate as a team?

Talking point

How did you help your team today?

Before you go

Which of the communication skills do you think was most useful in the team task? Take a vote.

2.2 Is it fair?

✓ **Collaboration**
✓ Communication
✓ Reflection

1 👥 💬 Look at the picture. Talk about what you can see.

2 👥 💬 What does fair mean? Give examples of things that are fair and unfair.

3 👥 💬 Read each statement and place it on the opinion scale. Do you all agree?

> I got told off for something I didn't do.

> Teachers spend the same time helping everyone in our class.

> At sports day, prizes are given to children who run the fastest.

> My best friend invited everyone in our class to her birthday party.

> My older brother gets more homework than me.

Opinion scale	Very unfair	Unfair	Neither	Fair	Very fair

4 📖 Read and respond.

Key term

opinion: a thought or belief about something, which cannot be proved to be true or false

EGG DROP TASK

The goal of this task is to **design and build something to protect an egg** that is dropped from a height. The **egg must be in perfect condition** at the end of the task. Each team will receive a top-secret task that gives more details. These tasks may give an advantage or a disadvantage.

a 👥 📖 💬 Read your task and discuss how you will carry it out.

b 👥 ✏️ Draw a diagram to show how you will protect your egg during the task.

This drawing shows the shape of the egg protection capsule. It shows what materials will be used.

c 👥 💬 Start constructing! Use the engineering design process model to help you work effectively in your group.

d 👥 Test your design to complete your mission.

Cotton wool

Egg

Balloons

Paper cone

THE ENGINEERING DESIGN PROCESS

DEFINE A PROBLEM

IMAGINE & PLAN

CREATE

TEST

IMPROVE

SHARE

5 👥 💬 **Reflect on the task. Discuss these questions in your teams.**

How successful was your team in completing the task?

What did your team do well?

How good was your team communication?

What could your team have done better?

How fair was this challenge and what effect did this have on the teams?

What have you learned about teamwork from this challenge?

It's not fair! Only the older children can bring their own snacks to school.

Talking point

Were there any disagreements today? If there were, why do you think they happened?

Before you go

Look at the opinion. Do you agree?

2.3 Put yourself in their shoes!

1 👥 💬 **What can you see in this picture?**

Money brings you happiness.

2 **Give your opinions.**

a 👥 💬 Read the statement. Do you agree? Give your opinion and your reasons.

b 👥 💬 Work in pairs. Choose a statement below. One of you should agree with the statement and the other should disagree, giving your reasons.

Red cars look better than blue cars.	My mum is the best cook.	Children are lucky to go to school.

3 📖 **Read and respond.**

> **Why do we need breaks at school?**
>
> Most children like break time. They love having free time and choosing how to use it. One child explained, 'It's the best part of the day. I get to play with my friends.'
>
> Not everyone likes breaks. Lots of children don't enjoy them. They don't know what to do. They wander around uncomfortably for 20 minutes. Other children find them too noisy and chaotic.

a 👥 💬 What is your opinion on break times?

b 👥 ✏️ Choose one opinion from the text. Write an explanation of it using Point, Evidence, Explain. Look at the example to help you.

Point	Evidence	Explain
Some children like break times because they like being with friends.	A child says: 'It's the best part of the day. I get to play with my friends.'	Break times are a time when children can talk and play with friends.

4 📖 **Prepare for a debate on break times. Read the text.**

A debate is an organised argument between two teams of people. They research and present different points of view. Debates always start with a statement. One team agrees with the statement. The other team disagrees.

Each team **introduces their main point of view**, then **provides facts** as **evidence**. The team **concludes with a summary** of their arguments.

The topic of your debate is: *All children should have an extra 15 minutes of break time in school every day.* It does not matter if you agree or not. It is your team's job to find information to support your side of the argument.

a 👥 💬 Answer the questions.
- What is a debate?
- How is a debate organised?
- What is the topic of your debate?

b 👥 💬 Your teacher will put you into groups and tell you what side of the debate you are on. What do you already know to support your side of the argument?

c 👥 📖 ✏️ Read the research you have been given. Then record information to support your argument.

Point	Evidence	Explain	Source
Some children get bored at break times.	In the text it says: They 'don't know what to do'.	Children can find breaks boring if they don't have imagination or don't have playground equipment.	Professor Hopscotch Education Researcher *Centre for Play Learning, 4 April 2023*

d 👥 💬 What other arguments can you think of to support your view in the debate?

5 👥 💬 **Now hold your debate.**

> **Key terms**
>
> **fact:** something that can be proved to be true
>
> **source:** the place where you have found information during research; include the title, author and date

Talking point

How useful were your research records in the debate?

Before you go

Has your opinion about break times changed? Discuss any new information that has influenced your opinions.

2.4 **Do we all agree?**

1 What is harmony? Write a sentence saying what it means to you. Share your responses. Do you all agree?

2 **Read and respond.**

In a group, there may be lots of different personalities. Some people are happy to talk about anything in front of anyone. Some people need more encouragement to join in. Some are very quiet and don't like speaking in a large group. But everyone has something to contribute. It is important that no one is left out. What do you think is the best way to make sure that everyone's ideas are heard?

a How confident are you with sharing your ideas?

b In pairs, write a list of the ways that we share ideas with each other.

3 **Use research to find out what children like most about school.**

Lots of people say your school days are the best days of your life. Researchers asked some children what they liked most about school. Here are some of their responses.

This information can be used to answer the research question: *What do children like most about school?*

a 🔁 💬 Study the table. The information provided by Aditi's and Leo's comments has been filled in. What information is given in Mustafa's and Erika's comments?

Comment	Learning	People	Facilities	Feelings
'I like school because I love seeing my **friends**.' *Aditi, aged 8*		✓ friends		
'I feel **safe** at school.' *Leo, 9*				✓ safe
'My school is like a **big family**. We all know one another and **care** for each other.' *Azim, aged 9*				
'I really love my **art lessons** every Monday. I get to be creative.' *Erika, aged 10*				

b 🔁 ✏️ Complete the table on the worksheet to record all the information from research.

c 🔁 💬 What did you find out that will help you to answer the research question? Decide if the information on the research table tells you what most children want from school.

4 👤 📖 ✏️ **Many schools have a mission statement. This is something that explains what the school stands for. Read the mission statement and then use your research to make a mission statement of your own.**

> ## MISSION STATEMENT
>
> Our purpose is to provide a safe and creative school climate by building positive relationships, resulting in high academic and social achievement for all students.

> **Vocabulary**
>
> **mission:** an important task that people are given to do

> ### Talking point
>
> How does your mission statement answer the research question?

> ### Before you go
>
> Compare your opinions about school with your research findings.

2.5 **Actively listening**

1 **How good are you at listening?**

a 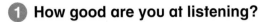 Read each statement. Write your response to each statement using the scale below, to find out what kind of listener you are.

1	I let people talk and I do not interrupt.
2	I try not to think about what I am going to say when someone is talking to me.
3	I give the person time to explore their ideas, thoughts and feelings.
4	After someone has finished talking, I ask questions to check that I have understood.
5	I try not to form an opinion until I have heard everything

Never	Sometimes	Often	Usually	Always

b What did the listening survey show you?

If you mostly replied *usually* or *always*, you are a good listener. A good listener is an *active listener*. That means you give your full attention and listen carefully. You think about what someone says and show your understanding. It's a great skill. It helps to build strong friendships.

2 **Play games to practise your active listening skills.**

Yes, but … game
Play in pairs. Choose one person to start.

The first person says: *The river is full of fish.*

The second person replies, with a sentence starting:
Yes, but … (for example, ***Yes, but*** *if it is full of fish there won't be anywhere for me to swim.*).

Take turns to build on each reply. Start each sentence with 'Yes, but …'.

a Follow the instructions to play the game in pairs.

b Now change the words from 'Yes, but …' to 'Yes, and …'. Repeat the conversation.

c Compare the two conversations. How did it feel to have your ideas accepted?

3 Look back at the activities you have done so far in this lesson.

   a 👥 ✏️ In pairs, write a list of things you need to do to listen well.

   b 👥 Use your list to create a poster. Use drawings and pictures to illustrate your poster.

4 📖 **Read and respond.**

At Montaz Primary School, we learn how to be active listeners. It's important because when we listen to each other, **it feels good**. It also helps us all to **be happy, safe and healthy**. It helps us to **get along** and **trust each other**. We are **kinder** and more **respectful** of our differences because we try to **understand one another**. We have become **more open-minded**. This means there are **fewer arguments**. If we do have problems, we can use our **listening skills** to help us **solve problems** by **ourselves**. When we listen to other people's ideas, we **learn from one another**.

   a 👥 💬 What would be a good title for this text?

   b 👥 ✏️ Write a list of the benefits of active listening.

5 👥 💬 **In pairs, tell each other what active listening is and what its benefits are. Use 'Yes, and …' to help each other improve your explanation.**

3 mins

Active listening feels good.

Yes, and …

Talking point

How successful were you at explaining active listening?

Before you go

How will you improve your listening in the future? Write a word or phrase to show what you want to improve.

2.6 Tell me how …

1 👥 💬 **How good are you at explaining?**
Tell a partner how a mobile phone works.
Try not to hesitate or repeat yourself.
You have one minute!

2 📖 **Look at the pictures.**

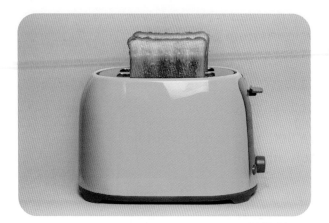

a   👥 ✏️ Choose an object. Write a short,
clear paragraph to explain how your object
works. Present your ideas logically. Only
include information that you think is important
and relevant.

b   👥 💬 Read out your explanations. How well
did you communicate?

3 📖 Read and respond.

Louis Braille

Children have made some important inventions. In 1824, Louis Braille developed a way for people to feel words. This gave people who could not see well an alphabet they could understand with their fingers. They were able to read, communicate and learn. This method for reading was named after him. It is called braille. At the time, Braille was only 15 years old.

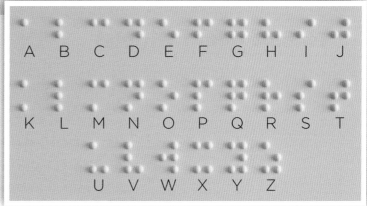

👥 💬 Answer the questions.

- How old was Louis Braille when he invented braille?
- What is braille?
- Who did his invention help?

4 📖 **Your teacher will give you a paragraph from a text about another young inventor. Use the information to complete the tasks.**

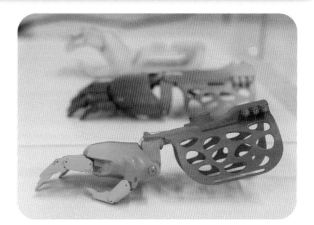

- a 👥 ✏️ Choose an appropriate method to record important facts from your text.

- b 👥 💬 Practise explaining your information in your group. Take turns to speak. Make sure that everyone understands the information.

- c 👥 💬 ✏️ Look at the worksheet. Fill in the gaps that you can from your own information. Then join a group to find the missing information. To fill in the rest, ask other groups questions. Organise your group to find the missing information.

Talking point

How well do you think you communicated today?

Before you go

What would you do to change the world?

2.7 How do you feel about change?

1 What does change mean to you? Use the word 'change' in a sentence.

2 Complete the questionnaire on the worksheet to find out how you feel about change. Tick 'yes' or 'no'. Share your responses.

3 Read and respond.

Change your attitude!

5 **Keep going:** Great! All I need to do now is keep it up!

4 **Action:** I am doing it. I'm making a change to reach my goal.

3 **Prepare:** I need to prepare and work out what I need to make my change happen.

2 **Think:** I understand that it's not too bad if I start doing things differently.

1 **Starting point:** I don't think I really need to change. Everything is fine …

a Talk about how you feel about change. Use your responses from the questionnaire to help you.

b Write statements that you can use to make positive change in your attitude to learning. Copy and complete the table.

Instead of …	Try thinking …
I'm not good at this!	What am I missing?
I'm great at this!	I am getting better at this.
I give up!	Maybe I could try again.
I can't make this any better.	
I made a mistake.	
She's so clever. I'll never be that clever.	
Plan A didn't work.	

4 📖 Read and respond.

a 👥 💬 What does the statement mean to you?

b 👥 💬 Look at the pictures below. How can you make a difference?

c 👥 💬 Choose one of the ideas and discuss what you would do with a partner. Explain what the result would be.

d 🧑 ✏️ Explain your idea. Use these questions to help you write about your action.

- What action do you suggest?
- How will you do it?
- Who will be affected by the outcome?
- How can this make a positive difference to a local issue?
- Why is it important?
- How does it change the world?
- What have you learned about how you can make a positive change?

> Small changes can make a big difference.

Talking point

What did you learn about your own attitudes to change?

Before you go

What positive changes do you want to see in the world?

2.8 **What change do they want?**

✓ Reflection
✓ Analysis

1 👥 💬 **What positive action has this boy taken?**

2 👥 💬 **Who do you know who has led actions for change?**

3 📖 **Read the quotation from Nickar Panyphorn, a 15-year-old girl. Then complete the tasks.**

Education is the mother of success. Today a reader, tomorrow a leader.

a 👥 💬 What does Nickar think will help people to succeed?

b 👥 📖 Read about Nickar. What positive action does she want?

Nickar Panyphorn

Nickar is from Lao People's Democratic Republic. Many children in Nickar's country do not go to school. About one in every five children does not go to primary school. Nickar believes education is important, and she wants to help make things better.

When she was small, she saw a young woman from school talk at the United Nations. She made it her goal to speak up for children. At 15, she achieved her goal. She spoke to world leaders at the United Nations about children's rights to education to tell them the importance of education. She asked world leaders to make policies so that no child was left behind.

After her speech, she became well known in her country. She joined a group of young people to discuss the challenges and find solutions to improve children's lives in Lao. They suggested improvements to the curriculum and things have already started to change.

Nickar believes her country will develop if more children go to school. She wants to see every child in her country wearing school uniforms, holding books and pens because a good education gives a better chance of success. Nickar is pleased that the number of children attending school is increasing and that schools are improving. She continues to be an active leader of change and speaks out for children in her country.

c ✎ Draw a flow chart to show Nickar's idea, action and its consequence.

| What did she want? | → | What was her action? | → | Who does her action help? |

4 📖 **Read about another young person who has made a difference.**

Mallayka Ianna Oddenyo (age 12, Kenya) started collecting plastic waste when she was eight. She saw a dead fish in a lake full of waste. This made her think about plastic pollution. Now, she collects and recycles plastic waste to make flower vases, picture frames, table mats, handbags and pencil holders. She also educates her community about reducing plastic waste and encourages young people to collect plastic. This stops plastic from going into oceans, lakes and rivers.

a 👥💬 Copy the table and use the coloured words to complete it.

Name	Problem	Action	**Result**

b 👤📖✎ Read the information on the worksheet. Add four more rows to your table and record the problem, action and result for each young person you have read about.

c 👤✎ Choose one of the actions from your completed table. Write a paragraph giving your opinion in a personal reflection. Use the questions below to help you.

Who did you find the most inspiring?

What inspired you about them?

What was their action?

What actions might you do as a result of reading about their action?

Talking point

How have these ideas influenced your own opinions or ideas?

Before you go

Which of these young leaders' actions do you prefer, and why?

Unit 2 Final task: Give a presentation about World Kindness Day

✓ **Communication**
✓ Research
✓ Reflection

Read the final task and discuss the question.

> Work in **teams** to **research** and **present** information **about World Kindness Day** to people in your **school community**. Explain **what** it is, and **how**, **where**, **who** and **why** it is celebrated. Finish your presentation with ideas for **positive actions** you would like to **introduce** to **promote kindness** in your school, using ideas gained from your **research**.

1 👥 💬 **What do you need to do to be successful in this task? Use the words in bold to help you.**

2 💬 **Share ideas about World Kindness Day.**

   a 👥 💬 What do you think happens on World Kindness Day?

   b 👥 ✏️ Write a list of questions to help with your research.

When was the first World Kindness Day?

When was the first ...?

3 📖 **Read some information about World Kindness Day. Then organise and complete your research.**

a 👥 ✏️ Find, select and record information. Copy and complete the table to answer your questions.

> World Kindness Day is an event that is celebrated every year on 13 November all around the world. The first World Kindness Day was held in 1998. It began because people wanted to raise awareness about kindness. The idea is that on this day, people think about being kind to one another and doing actions that spread kindness. In some countries, like Australia, it is so important that they make it a national holiday. Many schools add it to their calendars and organise special events to encourage kindness. In some countries, offices get involved. It is a day when people do good deeds for their communities, focus on positive thoughts and bring people together with kindness. It tries to involve everyone from all races and religions everywhere.

Question	Information
When did World Kindness Day begin?	1998

b 👥 💭 Is more research needed? Locate and record information for any unanswered questions. Use key words 'acts of kindness' to research actions.

Questions	Notes	Source
What do I still want to find out?		Where did I find the information?

4 👥 💭 **Choose a positive action to promote kindness in your school.**

- Use ideas from previous lessons in this unit.
- Explain your idea, action and its impact.

5 👥 💭 **Create your presentation. Explain your research and your ideas for actions.**

6 👥 💭 **Present your information about World Kindness Day.**

Top tips

- Research, plan and prepare your presentation to give a clear message.
- Use simple pictures for interest and keep texts short.
- Rehearse your points.
- Stay calm and take your time. Give your audience warmth, excitement and energy. Do not read from your slides.
- Check your work carefully.

Reflection: How successful was our presentation about World Kindness Day?

a   Complete the final task checklist. Use the worksheet.

b   Share your checklist with your team. Do you all agree?

Final task checklist			
We presented our information clearly.	☺	😐	☹
The action benefited our school community.	☺	😐	☹
We clearly explained the positive impact of our action.	☺	😐	☹
We showed evidence of research to support our ideas.	☺	😐	☹

c   Take turns to say what you did to help the team. Do you all agree?

d   Reflect on your what you have learned from this task. Complete the worksheet.

Before you go

Discuss these questions in pairs.

> What did you feel you did well in this task?
>
> What did you find most difficult in this task?
>
> What did you learn from this task?
>
> What have you learned from your research?
>
> What skills have you improved?
>
> How have your communication skills improved?
>
> What new methods have you learned or developed to record information?
>
> What skills do you need to practise?
>
> What will you do to be more successful next time?

Unit **3** Let's not waste it!

What do you know?

- How much food is wasted every year?
- What happens to food when you throw it away?
- Why does food waste affect our climate?

In this unit, you will:

- use different ways to communicate important messages about food waste
- design questionnaires to research a local issue
- explain how infographics can be used to spread awareness
- work in groups to solve food waste problems.

3.1 What a waste!

1 👥 💬 ✏️ **What do you know about food waste? Talk about the topic in pairs. Then copy the KWL chart and write what you know in the K column.**

K I know	W I want to know	L I learned

2 👥 ✏️ **What do you want to know? Add your questions to the 'W' column on the chart.**

3 👥 📖 💬 **Read the text. Does it answer your questions about food waste?**

What a waste!

Many of us don't have to worry about where our next meal will come from, but why do some people still go hungry? The world grows enough food to feed everyone in the world, yet not all the food produced makes it onto people's plates. A lot of food gets wasted. It is thrown away and ends up in landfill.

Food takes up more space than anything else in a landfill site. We throw away about 30–40% of all the food we grow. We need to throw away less. Farmers should try to grow only what they can harvest. Food should be stored and transported carefully so that it does not get damaged. Shops, homes and restaurants should use and buy only what they need.

Throwing away food is not just a waste of money. It is bad for the environment too. The gas that is made by rotting food is called methane, and it harms our planet. It is a greenhouse gas that traps heat around the Earth. Greenhouse gases stop the heat from escaping to space. This causes climate change and global warming. Throwing away food also wastes natural resources. Energy and people are needed to make, store, transport and cook food. It is important to sort out the food waste problem. If food is not needed, it can be reused to reduce the damage to our planet. It could be used as compost or burnt for energy.

Waste is usually crushed into small pieces and buried in landfills. Landfills are ugly and smell bad.

4 👤 ✏️ **Add to your KWL chart.**

K I know	W I want to know	L I learned
We waste food.	What happens to the food we waste?	30–40% food to landfill

a 👥 📖 Find the information from the 'L' column in the text you have just read.

b 👥 ✏️ Look at the questions you wrote for Activity 2. Can you find answers in the text? Write any answers in the 'L' column of your chart in note form. Use the Note-taking tips to help you.

c 👥 ✏️ Record any other information you have learned from the text.

d 👥 💬 What questions in your chart have not been answered?

Talking point

What did you learn about note-taking today? How good were you at making notes? Give yourself a ranking of 1 to 5, where 5 is the best.

Before you go

What positive actions can people do to reduce food waste?

3.2 Reduce food waste

1 👥 📖 💬 **Read the text. Rewrite the actions in bold to show a different consequence. Use the example to help you.**

> Sofiya and Anoushka buy some fruit. One banana has gone brown, so **they throw it away.**
>
> The children prepare a fruit salad using one banana, one apple and half the melon. It looks delicious so **they take a big helping.** They can't finish everything on their plate, so they **throw half an apple into the bin.** The rest of the **melon is left out on the side and spoils.**

One banana has gone brown, so **they throw it away.**

One banana has gone brown, so **they use it to make a milkshake.**

2 **Identify actions to reduce food waste.**

a 👥 💬 Explain these actions to reduce food waste in your own words.

use before

❄️

freeze food

compost

take smaller portions

only buy what you need

b 👥 💬 Which of the actions do you do in your home?

3 **Sofiya's school is researching food waste. Her teacher has asked her to keep a log about food waste.**

> **Key term**
>
> **log:** a record of all details and events relating to a particular thing

Food waste log

Day	Meal	Food product	Amount	Reason for waste
Monday	breakfast	breakfast cereal	½ cup	too much
	snack	banana	1 cup	gone brown
	lunch	rice	½ cup	too much
	lunch	carrots	1 cup	overcooked
Tuesday	breakfast	breakfast cereal	½ cup	too much

a 👥 📖 What information does she record?

b 👥 ✏️ Write one thing you notice about Sofiya's food waste habits.

c 👥 💭 Name one action she could take to reduce her food waste.

4 📖 **Look at a different way to present the information in Sofiya's log.**

	Monday				**Tuesday**			
Food type	⚪	⚫	⚪	⚪		⚪	⚪	⚪	
Amount of food wasted (cups)	½	1	½	1		½	1	2	
Reason for waste	P	S	P	D		P	D	P	

a 👥 💭 Answer the questions.

- What food type is wasted most?
- How many cups of food does Sofiya waste on Tuesday?
- What is the most common reason for her food waste?

b 👤 ✏️ Complete the table on the worksheet to show Sofiya's food waste over the week.

5 📖 **Read the statement Sofiya wrote about her food waste habits. Then complete the tasks.**

I wasted a total of 3½ cups of grain on Monday and Tuesday because my portion sizes were too big. If I take smaller portions, I will waste less food.

Key

Reasons for food waste:
P = portion size (too much)
S = spoilt food
D = didn't like
Food types:
⚪ grains
⚫ fruit
⚪ vegetables
⚪ dairy
⚪ protein foods

a 👤 ✏️ Write two more statements using information from your research record to explain your findings.

b 👥 💭 Suggest an action to help Sofiya.

Talking point

How useful did you find the key in Activity 4 for recording your notes?

Before you go

What will you do in your home to reduce food waste?

3.3 A global problem

1 **Can you eat the stickers on fruit?**

a 👥 💬 Take a class vote.

b 👥 💬 Who would you trust to give you this information?

c 👥 💬 How could you find out if this information is true?

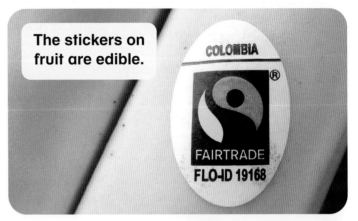

The stickers on fruit are edible.

COLOMBIA

FAIRTRADE
FLO-ID 19168

2 📖 **Look at this food fact. Read about the author.**

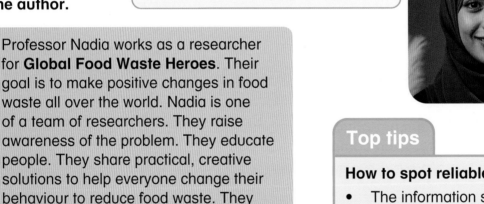

Did you know that 33% of all the food produced in 2022 was wasted?

Professor Nadia works as a researcher for **Global Food Waste Heroes**. Their goal is to make positive changes in food waste all over the world. Nadia is one of a team of researchers. They raise awareness of the problem. They educate people. They share practical, creative solutions to help everyone change their behaviour to reduce food waste. They organise events to inform, share recipes and provide ideas for schools.

a 👥 💬 Why do you think the author shared this food fact?

b 👥 📖 Read the tips about how to check information for research. Check the reliability of the food waste fact using the information given.

Top tips

How to spot reliable sources

- The information should be up to date.
- The author should be a trusted authority on the subject you are researching.
- The sources the author used should be easy to find, clear and **unbiased**.
- You should be able to find the facts in other sources.

Key terms

bias: a strongly held opinion that is influenced by experiences; people can show bias when they believe something is one way, even if it is not accurate

unbiased: fair; not affected by someone's opinions

3 📖 **Look at this infographic, read the information, then answer the questions.**

National Environment Organisation
Earth Day Every Day

FOOD WASTE HABITS   *NEO Consumer Survey 2022*

Actions to reduce food waste	Attitudes towards food waste

71% of people use up leftovers (up from 58% in 2020).	8 out of 10 people don't like uneaten food being thrown away.

64% of people have no leftovers when they eat out (up from 45% in 2020).	8 out of 10 people know that food waste is bad for the environment.

The **National Environment Organisation (NEO)** is a public national organisation. It is responsible for helping to build a clean, sustainable environment for present and future generations.

a 👥💬 Who produced this information? Use the Top tips on page 46 to decide how reliable the source is.

b 👥💬 How did the author get these facts?

4 📖 **Read and respond.**

a 👥💬 Look at the full infographic on the worksheet. The **survey** compares habits between 2020 and 2022. Find and discuss a positive change in behaviour about leftovers.

b 🧍✏️ Answer the questions on the worksheet.

> **Key term**
>
> **survey:** a way to find out information from a lot of different people by asking them all the same question

Talking point

Do you think this information could be true everywhere in the world? Discuss how you could find out.

Before you go

How do you think the problem in one country affects another?

3.4 Attitudes

1 📖 **Read and respond.**

a 👥 ✏️ In pairs, list all the different ways you can think of to reduce food waste. Use the pictures to help you.

b 👥 ✏️ For each of the tips you listed, discuss with your partner why people might *not* be able to do it. What solutions can you think of?

2 📖 **Look at the food waste word cloud.**

a 👥 📖 Read about why people use word clouds. Why are some words bigger than others?

Word clouds

Charts, graphs and infographics are a quick and easy way to show patterns in numerical (number) data. If the information collected is in words, researchers need to show these patterns in a different way. They can use word clouds. Word clouds work in a simple way: the more a word appears in a text, the bigger and bolder it appears in the word cloud.

b 👥 ✏️ Write down the five most important words in the word cloud.

3 📖 **Read about the London Environment Institute. Then answer the questions.**

London Environment Institute: using science to make a better tomorrow

We are an international **not-for-profit** research and policy organisation based in the UK. Our researchers are international experts in environmental science. Our research is used to advise policy-makers in government. We **find and offer solutions** for the **environmental challenges** faced by different countries and the world as a whole. We want to build a better tomorrow.

Do you think this organisation is a reliable source of information on food waste? Give reasons for your answer.

4 👥 📖 **The London Environment Institute carried out some research to understand why people waste food. They used the responses to their survey to make a word cloud. Look at the word cloud on the worksheet, then complete the tasks below.**

a 👥 💬 Match the words with their meaning.

supporting factor   an obstacle that stops you doing something

motivating factor   something that helps you to do something

barrier   a reason to do something

b 👥 ✏️ Use the information to complete the gap-fill on the worksheet.

Talking point

Compare the infographic from Lesson 3.3 with the word cloud. Which information do you find easier to analyse?

Before you go

Write down one thing you should check when deciding on the reliability of an information source.

3.5 Surveying food waste

1 😯 💬 **Why do you think food is often wasted in schools?**

2% of food waste in the USA comes from public schools.

16.5 kg per student per year

Increasing lunch times by 10 minutes cuts food waste by a third.

Source: 2022 National Farm to School Network

2 📖 **Read this comment by children at a primary school.**

Too much food is wasted in our school. We have learned that this is bad for our planet. We need to do something about it.

Key terms

questionnaire: a set of questions created to find out what people think about a topic

investigation: the process of collecting, analysing and interpreting data

a ✏️ Define the problem. Make notes under the following headings:

Purpose   Target audience   Use   Want to know.

b Suggest a research question the children could use to find out more about the problem.

c 😯 💬 Look at the stages of designing a questionnaire. What order do you think they should be in?

Test questions: Try out the questionnaire on a small group.

Write the questionnaire: Write questions for the **investigation**.

Define the problem: Decide what you want to find out. Write a research question.

Plan the investigation: Give details of the process. Decide how information will be collected, analysed and interpreted.

Question check: Check that questions are suitable and well written.

3 👥 📖 💬 **Study the students' plan for the investigation. Find the information in the planning sheet that explains *who*, *how*, *why*, *where* and *what* they will ask.**

Investigation planning sheet
What is the purpose of the investigation? *We would like to understand the food waste problem in our school.*
We want to find out … *The reasons that children waste food at school.*
Our research question is … *Why do children waste food at our school?*
We will collect our data by observation/(questionnaire).
We will question *50* people.
We will ask … *children aged 7 or over*
We will collect data by … *asking children face to face.*
We will conduct our investigation in (place) … *the lunchroom.*
We will record our data by … *completing questions on a questionnaire.*
The information will be used to … *raise awareness and change habits.*

4 **Choose the best questions.**

a 👥 💬 Should the students write **open questions** or should they write **closed questions**? Use their meanings in the Key terms box to help you decide.

b 👥 Help the group to choose good questions for the questionnaire. Sort the questions on the worksheet into closed or open questions.

> **Key terms**
>
> **open question:** a question where the person asked can give any answer they want; open questions often ask for reasons, explanations and descriptions
>
> **closed question:** a question where the person is asked to choose from one of several given answers; this makes information quicker to collect and the limited choice makes responses easier to analyse

Talking point

What have you learned about choosing questions for questionnaires?

Before you go

Why do you think researchers test their questionnaires?

3.6 **Let's investigate!**

1 Look at the picture.

a 👥 💬 What is the boy with the clipboard doing?

b 👥 💬 What other ways can data be collected?

c 👥 💬 What do you think are the advantages and disadvantages of each method of data collection?

2 ✏ **Write questions to investigate food waste using the research question.**

> Why do children waste food at school?

a ✏ Write a question that helps you to understand *what* people throw away.

b ✏ Write a question about food waste that asks for responses using a scale.

c ✏ Write a question about *how* food is wasted, which children can answer with 'yes' or 'no'.

d ✏ Write a question that helps you find a solution to the problem.

3 👥 💬 **Now discuss how you would organise your research.**

a Where you think the best place would be to ask your questions?

b How many children do you think you should ask?

c How much time do you think you will need to ask your 4 questions?

d How should you record your responses?

4 👥 💬 ✏️ **Ask your questions to children in your class and record your responses. Then write a statement to answer the following questions. Use the examples to help you.**

What did you find out?

E.g. We found out that most children …

How will you show the results of your questionnaire?

E.g. We used a tally chart to record our results and we decided to show our results for each question in pie charts.

Did your questions answer your research question?

Yes, we found out that … and this answered our research question because …

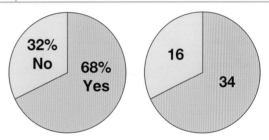

Would you use a compost bin at school?	
Yes	🪦🪦🪦🪦🪦🪦 IIII
No	🪦🪦🪦 I

How could you improve your questionnaire?

5 👥 **Share your results in a report.**

   a 👥 ✏️ Write a statement for each question to explain what you found out.

   b 👥 ✏️ Use your statements to write a team report of the investigation. Use the checklist for features of report writing to help you.

Talking point

How successful was your team report at answering the research question?

Checklist

Report features checklist

✓ A title and opening sentences clearly explaining what the report is about

✓ Paragraphs of information for each of the headings

✓ Tables/pictures/diagrams to add information

✓ Facts linked within each paragraph

✓ A conclusion – summary of key points

✓ Factual language

Before you go

What do you think is the best way to share awareness in the school community about this issue?

3.7 The food journey

1 😯 💭 **What do you think the phrase 'field to fork' means?**

2 **What happens to food?**

a 😯 💭 Use the diagram to describe each stage of the journey of food.

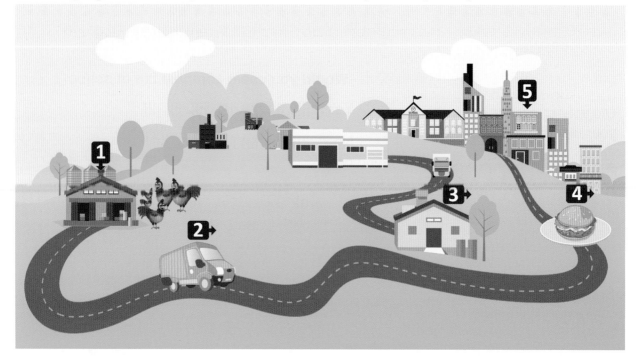

b 👤 ✏️ Add notes to the food journey diagram on the worksheet to explain each stage.

c 😯 💭 Look at the flow chart. In pairs, discuss how food might be wasted at each stage in the process.

The wasted food journey

On the farm 11% is lost. → After harvest 8% is lost. → During processing 1% is lost. ↓ In markets or stores 6% is wasted. → At home or in restaurants 10% is wasted.

d 👤 ✏️ Add notes to the diagram to show how food is lost.

3 📖 **Look at this infographic and complete the tasks.**

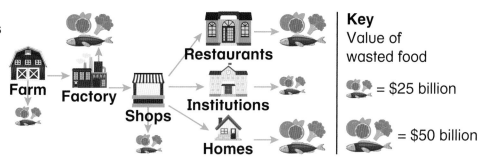

Farm **Factory** **Shops** **Restaurants** **Institutions** **Homes**

Key
Value of wasted food

🥦 = $25 billion

🥦🥦 = $50 billion

a 👥 💬 Use the key and image to explain how it is different from the diagram in Activity 2.

b 👤 ✏️ Add more details to your food journey diagram on the worksheet to show how food is wasted.

4 👥 💬 **How could you explain this information to young children?**

The children in Year 1 are learning about food waste. Their teacher would like your help to explain how food is wasted from field to fork. Your presentation will need to be clear, simple and fun. They would love it if you could use songs, stories or pictures.

a 👥 💬 Plan your performance. Use the pictures for ideas. Finish with an action that shows how to reduce food waste.

b 👥 👆 Practise your performance!

c 👥 Watch the performances. How successful were they? Use the Top tips to reflect on how successful your own performance was.

Top tips

- Keep it short and simple.
- Make it understandable, clear and factual.
- Engage with your audience!

Talking point

How successful was your team in communicating your message about food waste?

Before you go

How would you change your presentation if you were communicating with an adult in your family?

3.8 Super food savers

✓ **Collaboration**
✓ Communication
✓ Reflection

1 Meet Captain Greens. How could this character be used to raise awareness?

Captain Greens is on a **mission**. She travels the world saving imperfect vegetables from landfill. She flies into schools to talk to kids. She tells them about their superhero powers to save food and waste less.

2 Read and respond.

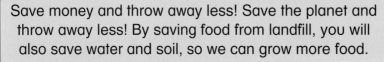

Save food, save the planet!
It's Captain Greens ...

Hi kids!, It's Captain Greens here, reporting for duty! Do you know how you can waste less food at lunch?

... and her sidekick, Broccoli Woman!

Save money and throw away less! Save the planet and throw away less! By saving food from landfill, you will also save water and soil, so we can grow more food.

TIPS TO BE A SUPER FOOD SAVER
- Feed yourself: Eat the food you take. Take only the food you will eat.
- Feed others: Food is for sharing. Share the food you can't eat. Start a food share table at school to encourage others.
- Feed the soil: Throw food scraps into a compost bin so it can help to build healthy soil.

a What is Captain Greens' message?

b It is important that information can be quickly, easily and clearly understood. Find examples of clear communication in the poster. Explain how they get the message across.

c Use the communication Top tips on page 55 to explain why cartoons are often used in awareness campaigns.

3 👥 💬 **Look at the cartoon. Discuss how this cartoon communicates the message of food waste in schools.**

4 In teams, create a cartoon to show other ways that families can reduce food waste at home. You will each draw one frame of the story. You will need to communicate your ideas clearly before you start. After you have agreed your plan, you will not be able to discuss your ideas with members of your team and you will need to work at a distance from your team mates.

a 👥 💬 What do you need to decide before you start?

b 👥 ✏️ Agree on your ideas and write them down. Use the questions in Activity 3 to help you. What will happen? Sketch the story.

5 👥 ✏️ 💬 **Now create your cartoon. Draw your own picture without talking to other members of your team. Then put your drawings together to tell the story.**

Talking point

How could you improve communication in your team?

Before you go

What other examples can you think of when teams of people might need to work together from a distance?

Unit 3 Final task:
Prepare an awareness campaign about food waste

Read the final task and discuss the question.

Work in **teams** to **investigate** the **food waste problem** in your school. Use your **research** to build **awareness** in your **school community** and suggest **an action** that will **reduce the problem.** You can raise awareness with a poster, leaflet, cartoon or a performance. You should **use facts** from your research to support your campaign. **Reflect** on your **teamwork skills**.

1 👥 💬 **What do you need to do to be successful in this task? Use the words in bold to help you.**

2 **Share what you know.**

   a 👥 💬 What do you know about the food waste problem at your school?

   b 👥 ✏️ Write a list of ways you could raise awareness about a problem.

   c 👥 📖 Read the Top tips to raise awareness. Decide how you will present your research findings to raise awareness and suggest an action to solve an issue in your school community.

Top tips

Tops tips to raise awareness
- Do your research.
- Know what you want to do.
- Understand your public.
- Take ideas from others.
- Use a familiar figure to support ideas.
- Spread your message widely.
- Have fun and engage your audience.

3 👥 **Plan your research.**

a 👥 💬 Discuss and agree on a good research question for your investigation.

b 👥 ✏️ Write a plan for your investigation, using the investigation planning template from Lesson 3.5. Remember to include details about how you will present your awareness campaign.

c 👥 💬 Compare your ideas with the food waste questionnaire investigation from Lesson 3.6. How will you need to change the questions to suit your plan?

4 👥 ✏️ **Write your questionnaire. When you have finished, check to make sure your questions match your purpose and the information you need.**

5 👥 **Conduct your research.**

a 👥 💬 Organise your team to collect, record and analyse your research data.

b 👥 👆 Complete your investigation.

c 👥 ✏️ Record and analyse your results.

d 👥 💬 Discuss your findings.

6 👥 **Communicate to raise awareness.**

a 👥 ✏️ Review your awareness campaign plan. Agree how you will use your research to raise awareness.

• Give a clear, simple message to raise awareness of the issue

• Suggest a positive action to reduce food waste

• Use facts to support your actions

• Engage your audience

b 👥 ✏️ Create your awareness campaign.

c 👥 💬 Present your awareness campaign with other groups.

Reflection: How successful was our campaign about food waste?

a   Complete the final task checklist. Use the worksheet.

b   Share your checklist with your team. Do you all agree?

Final task checklist			
We provided facts to support our actions.	🙂	😐	☹️
Our awareness campaign was clear and engaging.	🙂	😐	☹️
The action made a positive difference to a local issue.	🙂	😐	☹️
Team members contributed equally to the task.	🙂	😐	☹️

c   Take turns to say what you did to help the team. Do you all agree?

d   Reflect on your team's performance. Answer the questions on the worksheet.

Before you go

Discuss these questions in pairs.

What did you enjoy most about this task?

What did you find most difficult about this task?

How aware were you of the food waste problem at the start of the unit?

What information surprised you the most?

How have your attitudes towards food waste being influenced by this unit?

Unit 4 — Why do you want that?

What do you know?

- What influences your shopping choices?
- How has the way we shop changed?
- How is research used to help sell products?

In this unit, you will:

- look at different ways data can be used to understand shopping habits
- use research questions to help solve problems in business
- find out how shops and sellers get your interest
- understand what can affect shopping decisions.

4.1 How do you choose things?

1 👥 💬 **Choose the pen you prefer. Explain why you chose it.**

2 **Look at the picture of a remote-controlled robot. Complete the tasks.**

a 👥 💬 Who do you think would buy this? Why?

b 👥 ✏️ Make a list of the questions a buyer might have.

> How much does it cost?

3 📖 **Ahmed's mother wants to buy a toy robot for his birthday. These are the things she will look at to help her decide.**

- **Price:** How much does it cost?
- **Material:** What is it made of?
- **Quality:** How well is it made?
- **Ease of use:** How easy is it to use?
- **Fun factor:** How fun would it be to play with?

a 👥 💬 Compare this list with the one you wrote in Activity 2. Did you think of the same things?

b 👥 ✏️ Which factor do you think is the most important? Put them in order, from most to least important.

c 👥 💬 Compare your responses with another pair. Do you all agree?

d 👥 💬 Read how Ahmed's mother made her choice. Do you think Ahmed would have made the same choice? Why?

> Most important for me was a good price, but I also chose this robot because it was well made.

4 **Now think about another product – shoes!**

a 👤 👥 ✏️ What factors might someone consider when buying a pair of shoes? Write a list. Compare it with a partner.

b 👥 💬 Would you put comfort first? Take a vote.

5 📖 **Read and respond.**

Shoe shopping choices

60% of people aged **over 40** choose comfort when buying a shoe.

8 out of 10 teenagers choose their shoes according to **brands**.

30% of people say they would pay more for shoes made of a **sustainable** material.

45% of **under 40s** do **not put comfort at the top of their list**.

Nearly **5 in 10 parents** buy **designer** shoes for their children.

Black is the most popular colour for adult shoes.

On average, shoppers buy **3 pairs of shoes every year**.

3 out of 10 shoppers say they buy shoes in a sale.

Most children **under the age of 10** say they prefer colourful shoes.

Source: MarketRite: Leading Independent Consumer Research since 1989 (April 2023)

a 👥 💬 Answer the questions.

• Who might find this information helpful?

• Who was surveyed?

• What did they want to find out?

b 👥 ✏️ Answer the questions on the worksheet to identify patterns in buying choices.

Talking point

Were you a good listener today? Talk about something you heard in this lesson that you will remember. Why will you remember it?

Before you go

How do your buying choices compare with others?

4.2 How do you shop?

1 **Where do you shop?**

  a 👥 💬 Talk about a recent shopping experience you had with your family.

  b 👥 💬 How many ways to shop can you think of?

2 📖 **Read and respond.**

> In the past, people shopped in markets or small local shops. They mostly bought essential items. Today, people often buy more of what they want rather than what they need. There is more choice and more ways to buy things. People can shop online from their homes and choose products from all over the world. The connections between people and places across the planet have increased. We call this **globalisation**. It is all about a worldwide network of communication, transportation and trade.

  a 👥 💬 How have people's shopping habits changed?

  b 👥 💬 How does your family shop?

3 📖 **Look at the bar chart.**

  a 👥 💬 Describe what you notice.

  b 👥 💬 Who do you think might be interested in this information?

Number of people who buy products online worldwide

Number of people (billions) / Years

- 2017: 1.3
- 2018: 1.45
- 2019: 1.55
- 2020: 1.7
- 2021: 1.9
- 2022: 2

4 📖 **Read and respond.**

Click to shop! Many people find shopping online an easy way to shop.

 Baby Boomers (age 55–74) 41%

 Millennials (age 18–39) 67%

 Gen X (age 40–54) 56%

 Seniors (age 75+) 28%

  a 👥 ✏️ Answer the questions.

- What age group is least likely to shop online?
- What do you notice about the age of online shoppers?
- Why do you think one age group shops more online than another?

  b 👥 💬 Discuss how this research could be used to decide which products are sold online.

5 What affects people's buying decisions?

a 🔲 💭 Look at the pictures. What items might someone prefer to buy from local shops or markets?

b 👥 📖 Look at the infographic. It shows what attracts people to the products they buy. How do you think this could affect where certain products are sold?

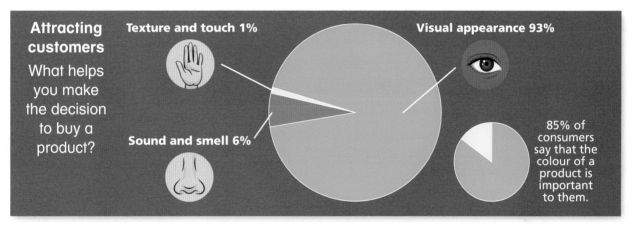

Attracting customers

What helps you make the decision to buy a product?

Texture and touch 1%

Sound and smell 6%

Visual appearance 93%

85% of consumers say that the colour of a product is important to them.

c 👥 ✏️ Use the infographic to answer these questions.

● Which sense do shoppers use most when buying products?

● How important is the feel of something when people are choosing a product?

● What are 85% of people most influenced by?

6 👥 💭 ✏️ A company making jackets has asked for your help to sell them to young people. Give the company advice, using the research you have analysed in this lesson.

a 👥 💭 Discuss how you would present your written response.

b 👥 ✏️ Write three statements to give the company some advice.

Talking point

How good are you at explaining data? Rate yourself from 1 to 5, where 5 is the best.

Before you go

Why do companies use market researchers to find out about people's buying habits?

4.3 Who can I trust?

1 Are these statements facts or opinions? Use the picture to write some facts and opinions of your own.

Facts tell us what happened. They can be proven to be true or false. **Opinions** are attitudes or judgements that cannot be proven. Knowing the difference can help you to decide how much you can trust the information.

These shoes are blue.

These shoes are cool!

2 Read and respond.

FITNESS*feet* shoes are made for walking! After experiencing their amazing cushioned soles, you will never want to walk in anything else. They are a real bargain at only $15 a pair. Buy them in all good stores.

a Find one fact and one opinion in the statement.

b Look at the statements about FITNESS*feet* on the worksheet. Are they facts or opinions? Complete the table.

3 An organisation called WIFS has written an article to help parents choose shoes for their children. Would you trust their advice? Why, or why not?

What is WIFS?

The World Institute of Foot Specialists (WIFS) started in 1949 by medical experts. We now have more than 7800 members worldwide. We advise companies and communities. We provide an educational programme for our members and educate our patients to improve foot health.

4 📖 **Read and respond.**

Back-to-School Shopping Tips

Before you head out to buy new shoes for your kids, read this …

Shoes should fit: Best fit is a finger's width from the end of the tip of the big toe. A little big is OK, but too big and the foot will slide. Too small and your child might get blisters.

Shoes wear out: Check your child's shoes regularly. Worn-out shoes give less support, leading to damaged ankles and heels.

Flat feet: Children with flat feet need a shoe with a wide toe box, arch support and shock absorption. The best shoes are lace-ups that have space for an orthopaedic insert, if needed.

For more information, search WIFS Foot health facts

a 👥 💬 What is the purpose of this information?

b 👥 💬 How can you decide if this source is reliable? Use the checklist to help you.

c 👥 ✏️ Select and copy evidence from the text to answer the questions on the worksheet.

Checklist

Reliable sources checklist

✓ **Is the author an expert?** Look at who they are and their qualifications.

✓ **Is the information factual?** Look out for opinions.

✓ **Is the information objective?** Watch out for people trying to sell you something!

✓ **Can you check the information in another source?** Decide if you can find this information elsewhere.

✓ **Is the information up to date?** Consider if this information could have changed.

Talking point

What have you learned today about checking sources?

Before you go

What might make a source unreliable?

4.4 What sources can we trust?

1 📖 **Read and respond.**

> A primary source is original information. It is by someone who was involved in the event being studied. Some primary sources give facts about a subject and some give a point of view. A secondary source does *not* give original information. It usually gives a report or summary of a primary source.

a 👥 💬 Explain the main difference between a primary and a secondary source in your own words.

b 👥 💬 Look at the pictures. Which is the primary source and which is the secondary source?

c 👥 💬 Which do you think is the most reliable source?

2 👥 ✏️ **Look at these different sources of information. Sort them into primary and secondary sources.**

Doctor

Farmer

Newspaper

School receptionist

Book

Your best friend

3 📖 **Look at these lists of information and sources.**

One cow can produce 22 litres of milk a day.

The age you said your first words.

Running shoes need to be comfortable and have cushioned soles.

The first sign of measles is a flat, red rash.

Olympic marathon runner

Doctor

Parents

Farmer

a 👥 💬 Who would be the most reliable source for each piece of information?

b 👥 💬 Use the Reliable sources checklist in Lesson 4.3 to explain how else you could check the reliability of a source.

4 👥 📖 💬 **Read an article published last week in *Review Weekly* magazine. Do you think this information is reliable? Why, or why not?**

═══════ Summer running shoes: best buys ═══════

We've been road-testing some kids' running shoes on our mini-testers aged between two and ten, taking them to school, to the park, off-road – everywhere, really. Get the perfect running shoe. Read our reviews and follow our expert's advice.

'Choose a running shoe that is comfortable, fits well, is safe and long lasting. Don't let your feet slip about in badly fitting shoes. Buy shoes with secure fastenings like laces or Velcro.'

Dr Lee, The Foot Clinic Founding Member of World Institute of Foot Specialists (WIFS)

GTEC Minis
Best: Overall ⭐⭐⭐⭐⭐

We normally say buy less, buy better, but this shoe is a bargain. Our eight-year-old tester just didn't want to take them off. Lightweight, extra grip and a Velcro fastening, they're designed for kids of all ages. Their bright colour makes them stand out. A great deal at only $30.
Click to buy now

Little Dynamo
Best: Look ⭐⭐⭐⭐⭐

These fabulous running shoes just light up the room. Our little testers loved the lights that flashed as they ran. An added feature is the on/off switch for the light sensors. This makes this new edition a much more popular choice for active school wear! Your kids will love these delightful flashy shoes! Worth the money at only $100.
Click to buy now

5 👤 ✏️ **Check the reliability of the source. Use the worksheet.**

Talking point

How good are you at evaluating sources?

Before you go

Suggest something you should check when evaluating sources.

4.5 **Reading pictures**

1 How are pictures used in different sources?

a 👥 💬 What is happening? Describe how it makes you feel.

b 👥 💬 What information do these pictures give? Match the source with their purpose.

FINANCIAL AND BUSINESS NEWS

- ADVERT -

Inform about what is happening in the world

Explain a fact

Sell something

Share something they have done

2 👥 📖 **Why do you think it is important to be visually literate? Read and discuss how images are used to communicate.**

Pictures can be very powerful. They can help us to communicate, exchange ideas and find our way in the modern world. Images surround us in our daily lives – from screens to billboards – yet we don't always think about how we use and understand them. We need to be aware how the images we see might try to affect how we think or might be used to make us believe something that is not true. Just as people learn to read and write words, people can learn to read, write and create strong images. This is called 'visual literacy'.

3 What does this image say to you?

a 88 💬 Describe what you see in the picture.

b 88 💬 What do you think has happened?
How is the girl feeling?

c 88 💬 Share your ideas. Do you all agree?

4 📖 Study the ideas map.

Camera angle: Gives the point of view.

Body language: Shows the feelings and relationship between people.

Colour: Expresses emotions and feelings.

Framing: Frames objects to show their importance.

Visual literacy

Positioning: Shows the connections between different elements.

Highlight: Draws your eye to objects in the picture through colour, place or focus.

Movement: The eyes of the subject direct you to the action.

a 88 💬 What does a photographer use to make you feel part of the action?

b 88 💬 Describe the picture using one element of visual literacy.

> Her head is leaning to the side. She could be tired, sad or bored.

5 88 ✏️ Evaluate the picture. Answer the questions on the worksheet. Then write a few words or phrases to add to the image to communicate a message.

Talking point

What have you learned about reading pictures?

Before you go

How can an image be used to communicate a feeling?

4.6 The value of pictures

1 Look at the picture. What is being advertised? Explain what you know about the product. Why would people want to buy this product?

2 Discuss (or make a list of) how the information is communicated using your knowledge of good communication skills.

3 📖 **Read and respond.**

Adverts need to make people want to read them. They should be **easy to read**, **simple** and **grab** your **attention quickly**. Think about **who** you want to sell to and work out **how** it will make them **really want** to own **the product**. **Promise** them something! Adverts should **give information** about the product. Use **powerful adjectives** to make the **benefits** of your product really **stand out**, but always **tell the truth**! And finally, to make it **memorable**, add a **catchy slogan** and your **brand name**.

a 👥 💬 What does the advertising company say makes a good advert?

b 👥 ✏️ Write a list of the features of a good advert.

Simple

Grabs attention quickly

c 👥 💬 How does the list you made about good communication in activity 2 compare with the information from the advertising company?

d 👤 ✏️ Share your ideas about good communication with another pair. Do you have the same ideas? You could use the worksheet.

4 👥 📖 **Read the design brief for a drinks brand. Use the advertising agency tips to create a successful advert. Include a drawing or find a suitable photograph. Be creative, keep it catchy and easy to read! Be ready to defend your advert to explain why it would appeal to your local market.**

Design brief

Our company **Chills**® is fast becoming a leading international drinks brand. You have been chosen to work on our design team! We would like your help to advertise our newest product in *your* country. *FruityChills*® – *Pick up and drink up!* – is a delicious, healthy drink made from only natural ingredients.

Talking point

What choices did you make to design a good advert? Why did you make them?

Before you go

What do advertisers need to think about when designing adverts?

4.7 **Asking the right questions**

1 👥 💬 Tyler's Toys has made toys for over 100 years, but nobody is buying the toys now. What do you think Mr Tyler should do?

> My toys aren't selling any more. People don't seem to like them. I don't know what to do!

> You don't **understand today's children**! Their toy habits have changed. You need to **find out what they want**. Then you can make toys they *will* buy and start selling them all around the world!

2 👥 💬 What skills do you think a researcher needs? Why is a research question like a lighthouse? Read to find out.

Secrets of success

If you want to succeed in business, you need to know your market. It's simple. Just do your research! Begin by deciding *what* you want to know. Be careful! It's a big world out there! Start thinking like a researcher. It's essential to focus your research and choose a good question. A good research question is like a lighthouse, it lights the way and guides your research. Get the research question right and you will be able to understand your problem.

3 📖 Look at the steps you should take to decide on a good research question.

a 👥 💬 Does Mr Tyler have enough information to start writing his research question?

b 👥 💬 How could he focus his research further?

The path to a good research question

Topic: What's the main area to be investigated?	School bags
Background information: What do we already know about the topic?	School bags are used by school children to carry things.
Focus: What exactly do we want to know?	The perfect size for school bags for five-year-old children.
Problem: What problem to we want to resolve?	The bag needs to be big enough for school equipment but light enough to carry.
Research question: Turn the problem into a research question.	What is the best size for a school bag for a five-year-old?

4 👥 📖 ✏️ **Help Mr Tyler find the best research question for his problem. Use the worksheet.**

Do children still play with toys?

Where do families buy their toys?

5 👥 ✏️ **Use this checklist to explain why Mr Tyler should reject some of his questions.**

a 👥 ✏️ Add reasons to the table on the worksheet to explain your responses.

b 👥 💬 Compare your responses with other groups. Do you agree?

Checklist

Research question checklist
- ✓ The question looks at a single problem.
- ✓ It is possible to check the information with research.
- ✓ It is easy to answer in the time you have.
- ✓ The question is easy to understand.
- ✓ The answer gives more than a few facts.
- ✓ The answer helps to understand the problem.

Talking point

How did you help your team find research questions today?

Before you go

What should Mr Tinker do next?

4.8 Know your business

1 👥 💬 **Imagine that you are going to set up a new business. What do you know about business? Tell a partner.**

2 📖 **Businesses offer services or products to people. Choosing the right product is essential to the success of a business. Read about 'Flaky Boots'.**

Flaky Boots' Business Flop

Flaky Boots are the leading maker of snow boots. When they learned that there were no snowshoes for sale in Fiji, they decided to open a shop there. After one year, they still hadn't sold one pair!

a 👥 💬 Learn from this company's mistakes. What went wrong for the Flaky Boots company?

b 👥 💬 Use the words in the Key terms box to suggest what the company should have done.

> **Key terms**
>
> **product research:** research to find out if a new product or service might be successful and how best to sell it
>
> **market research:** collecting information to help a company sell their products or services – who buys them and what they want

c   👥 🗨 Match the information with the headings to help Flaky Boots identify a research question.

TOPIC (product)	BACKGROUND INFORMATION What do you know already?	FOCUS What do you need to find out?	PROBLEM	RESEARCH QUESTION

The company does not know where people need snow boots.	Where is there a need for snow boots?	Warm boots used for walking in snow.	Snow boots	The places in the world where people want boots to walk in snow.

3 👥 🗨 **Choose your product from one of the options below. Then discuss what you want to know that could help you sell your product. Use the headings in the chart above to help you decide.**

- cars
- clothes
- toys
- pets

4 👥 ✏ **Use the worksheet to plan your research question.**

5 👥 🗨 **Use the Research question checklist from Lesson 4.7 to give feedback to another group about their research question.**

Talking point

What were the challenges and benefits of working in a team today?

Before you go

What do you think is the secret of a good business?

Unit 4 Final task:
Write a report evaluating an advert

Read the final task and discuss the question.

> Work in **teams** to **evaluate** the **advert** for a product of your choice.
> Use your visual literacy skills and understanding of adverts to evaluate
> the advert. **Write a report** to comment on its **purpose**, explaining its
> **strengths** and **limitations**. Use your knowledge of your own country to
> comment on how well the advert will work in your **local community**.

1 What do you need to do to be successful in the task?
Use the words in bold to help you.

2 Choose an advert that you like and start your research.

a Look at a selection of adverts and select one for the task.

b Make a list of reasons why it appeals to you.

3 **Evaluate your advert. Use what you have learned over the unit to help you.**

> What makes a good advert?

> Why might an advert be unreliable?

> Has the designer used visual literacy skills?

> What are the features of an advert?

> What do I know about the local market?

> Why might people need or want this product?

> What makes this advert grab your attention?

> What problems does this product promise to help you with?

> Would my local community like this product? Why? Why not?

a Decide together how you will evaluate your source. Make notes to plan your report. Use the worksheet.

b What is the local appeal of your advert?

> In your evaluation, it is important to think about how well an advert for a global brand can work in a local market. Consider what the places and people look like in the advert, and if it has the same interests and values as your local culture.

4 **Write your report.**

a Decide how you will organise your team to write the report. Use the structure of your plan to help you divide the task fairly.

b Use your notes in your report plan to write your report. Don't forget to check in with each other to review your work.

5 **Present your report. Give each team feedback on their report writing skills. Use the reflection prompts to help you.**

Reflection: How successful was our report?

a 👤✏️ Complete the final task checklist. Use the worksheet.

b 👥💬 Share your checklist with your team. Do you all agree?

Final task checklist			
The report was well-organised and clear.	🙂	😐	☹️
The evaluation commented on the author and purpose of the source.	🙂	😐	☹️
Strengths and limitations of the source were well explained.	🙂	😐	☹️
Comments were included about the local appeal of the source.	🙂	😐	☹️
Evidence from research was used to support ideas and opinions.	🙂	😐	☹️

c 👥💬 Take turns to say what you did to help the team. Do you all agree?

d 👤✏️ Reflect on your personal contribution. Answer the questions on the worksheet.

Before you go

👥💬 Discuss these questions in pairs.

What did you enjoy most about this task?

What did you find most difficult about this task?

Did you need any help during the task? If yes, who did you ask?

What have you learned in this unit?

What do you know?

- How have schools changed?
- Why do we need technology in schools?
- How do we use technology in the classroom?
- What will classrooms look like in the future?
- What do you think about the use of technology in schools?

In this unit, you will:

- use research questions to guide research into the history of learning
- practise note-taking to compare information about the uses of technology
- find and comment on different perspectives about the future of technology in schools
- design questionnaires to find opinions
- conduct investigations to understand what people think about technology.

5.1 Schools in the past

1 How do you think schools have changed since your grandparents went to school?

a Share what you know about schools in the past.

b How could you learn more about schools in the past? Name primary and secondary sources of information that could help you.

c What were you unsure about? Write a list of questions you could ask your parents or an older person you know.

When were computers first used in schools?

Key terms

primary source: information that comes directly from someone involved in the event being researched; it is original information that can be fact or opinion

secondary source: a report, summary or interpretation of information from a primary source; it does not give original information

2 **You are going to research schools in the past.**

a   Use the ideas map on the worksheet to create a list of subtopics that interest you about schools in the past.

b   Choose a subtopic from your ideas map that interests you. You will use this as a focus for your research.

3 **What are you curious about? Copy the KWL chart and add five questions to the W column to show what you want to know.**

K: What do you know?	W: What do you want to know?	L: What have you learned?
	What did they learn in maths lessons? What helped them to calculate difficult sums?	

4 **Use your notes to write a research question.**

a   Complete the flow chart on the worksheet to choose a research question.

b   Check and improve the quality of your research question. Use the Checklist to help you.

c   Present your research question to the class. Use the Checklist to explain why you think it is good.

Checklist

✓ The question looks at a single problem.
✓ You can check the information with research.
✓ It is easy to answer in the time you have.
✓ The question is easy to understand.
✓ The answer gives more than just a few facts.
✓ The answer helps to understand the problem.

Talking point

How have you improved your research question writing skills?

Before you go

How will you find out the answer to your research question?

5.2 What's changed?

1 👥 📖 **What interests Ali Gibra? Use the books he has been reading to suggest a topic he could research.**

2 Ali has started to do some background research for his project.

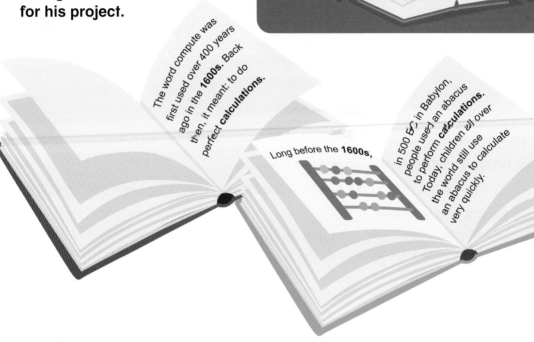

The word compute was first used over 400 years ago in the **1600s**. Back then, it meant: to do perfect **calculations.**

Long before the **1600s**,

in 500 *BC* in Babylon, people used an abacus to perform **calculations.** Today, children all over the world still use an abacus to calculate very quickly.

a 👥 💭 How is Ali's information connected?

b 👥 💭 Ali is interested in everything he is learning, but he has too much information. What should he do?

3 👥 📖 **Here are some of the interesting facts Ali has read. Help him to choose a focus for his research. What links all these facts?**

Early humans counted animals and other objects by carving tally marks into cave walls, bones, wood or stone. They made a mark for every item being counted. This system was useful for counting small numbers. As societies grew, however, there was a need for more complex ways to count, so numbers developed.

The most common number system used today is called the decimal system. It has 10 digits (0–9). They can be combined to write any number. It was invented by Hindus in ancient India. Later, Arabs improved the system. This is why we often call these modern numbers Hindu-Arabic numerals.

4 Help Ali to find a research question for his history project.

a 👥 ✏️ Write three more questions that Ali might have asked when he collected this information.

b 👥 💬 Choose the best research question for Ali. Use the checklist from Lesson 5.1 to explain why you chose it. Use the worksheet.

I want to know …

Where do numbers come from?

Who invented numbers?

5 Ali has chosen a research question. He has used his question to find key words to help him scan for information in books or online.

Research question: What is the <u>history</u> of the <u>numbers</u> used in <u>schools today</u>?

a 👥 ✏️ Copy the table. Put the words from the box in the correct column to match the key words. One example has been given for each key word.

history	numbers	school	today
past	digits	education	now

present   teach   numerals   ancient   decimal   learn   modern

b 👥 💬 Explain how these words helped Ali, using the example below.

The most common number system used <u>today</u> is called the <u>decimal</u> system. It has 10 digits (0 9). They can be combined to write any number. It was invented by Hindus in ancient India. Later, Arabs improved the system. This is the reason we often call these modern numbers Hindu-Arabic numerals.

c 👥 ✏️ Use your chosen research question to make your own table of key words on the worksheet.

d 👥 ✏️ Can you find any of your key words in the information Ali found? Use the worksheet.

Talking point

What skills did you learn today that will help you conduct research?

Before you go

How are research questions used to search for information?

5.3 Tomorrow's classroom

1 👥 ✏️ **Search for devices around your school. Look for computers, laptops, tablets, phones, cameras, and so on. Make a chart to record what you find.**

2 **How do you use technology?**

a 👥 ✏️ Make a list of all the ways you use technology, at home and at school.

b 👥 💬 How does technology help us to learn?

3 📖 **Read and respond**

The News Link

August 2023   **by Nathan Jobs**

Tech trends that will shape the education of tomorrow

To make learning fun, schools need to bring in more technology. They must look to the future and be positive about this change. Many schools are already thinking about new ways to learn in the classroom. Here are some of their top technology picks.

1 Smart device-based learning: Using these gadgets in the classroom is more fun. It keeps kids interested and they get instant feedback on their progress. Children become active learners. Smart devices also let them order and plan their tasks so they can choose when they study.

2 Interactive boards: These boards replace whiteboards or blackboards in the classroom. They connect with computers and show everything that's on a computer screen, from films to lessons to games. You can touch them like a tablet, which allows students to get more involved in the lesson.

3 Robotics lab: A robotics lab has programmable robots. Kids love them and they learn great programming skills. They can see the effects of their hard work in real time as they interact with their robots. This teaches them valuable skills for the workplace.

4 AI-based learning: These computer programs can change to suit the needs of the student. They find knowledge gaps and help them to practise skills they find difficult. They can also help people who speak different languages or have difficulty hearing or seeing. Teachers like them too because it helps them to understand their students better.

a What changes does the news report suggest?

b What is the writer's opinion of these changes?

4 **Record information to show the benefits of future technology.**

a What does the news report suggest smart devices do to improve learning? Find key words from the text to make notes to show the benefits.

b Select, organise and record the information from the report to show the benefits of the other trends in technology. Use the worksheet.

5 **Use the notes you made on the worksheet to explain each trend and the advantages stated in the news report. Which of these trends do you think will improve learning the most?**

Talking point

How helpful were your notes when you talked about technology trends in schools? What could you do to improve them next time?

Before you go

Can you think of any disadvantages to having more technology in the classroom?

5.4 Education is the future

1 😺 📖 💬 **Read the text. Answer the questions.**

- What is UNICEF?
- What does this organisation do?
- What issue is it trying to solve?

All about UNICEF

UNICEF is an aid organisation that helps to keep children safe in more than 190 countries around the world. It protects the rights of every child, everywhere. The work of UNICEF is guided by the UN Convention on the Rights of the Child (CRC). This is an agreed list of rights for all children around the world.

One of these rights is the right to education. UNICEF wants every child to have the chance of a good education, to be able to read and write. They want to make a difference in young people's lives. Their projects aim to get every young person in school, learning, training or employed by 2030.

Although the numbers of children who go to school has increased over the past few decades, about 60 per cent of primary school children in developing countries still cannot read or write. This means they do not have the skills they need to get jobs in the modern world. UNICEF want poor children to get the opportunities that richer children enjoy.

---

2 **What do you know about education around the world?**

a 😺 ✏️ Make a list of reasons that some children might not go to school.

b 😺 💬 Why do you think it is important for children to go to school?

3 📖 **Read and respond.**

> **Access to water gives kids time in school**
>
> When children **don't have water** at home, they often need to collect it for their families. Children around the world spend 200 million hours each day collecting water. This **takes time away from school**.

a 👥 💬 Explain the problem.

b 🧍 ✏️ Record the issue and its consequence in the table on the worksheet.

Access to water	What are the consequences?
Children don't ...	This means that ...

4 📖 **Read and respond.**

> ## Safe water improves the lives of poor families
>
> The time that was spent collecting water can be spent working or growing food for their families.
>
> This helps them to grow **10% more food** and **stops 150 million people from going hungry**.
>
> Children **attend school more** *and* **do better** because they are less hungry.
>
> If children do better in school, they will get **better jobs** and make **more money** in the **future**.

a 🧍 ✏️ Use the information to complete the table on the worksheet to show the positive consequences of access to water.

b 👥 💬 Use your notes to explain the issue and compare the consequences of having or not having access to water at home.

c 👥 💬 Share your opinions on what you have learned today.

Talking point

How did your notes help you today?

Before you go

How does your school prepare you for a job in the future?

5.5 Teachers of the future

✓ **Evaluation**
✓ Analysis
✓ Reflection

1 😃 💬 **How did you learn to read? Talk about the people or things that helped you.**

2 **What makes a good teacher?**

   a 😃 💬 Tell a partner words you could use to describe a good teacher.

   b 😃 ✏️ Write a description of a good teacher.

3 **Look at this magazine headline, then answer the questions.**

Will robots replace teachers?

   a 😃 💬 Rob Otis has been a teacher all his life. Why has this magazine headline upset him?

   b 😃 💬 Do you agree that robots could replace teachers? Choose a number from the scale to show how much you agree with the statement.

Strongly disagree	Disagree	Neither agree nor disagree	Agree	Strongly agree
1	2	3	4	5

4 😃 📖 **Read the first part of the magazine article. Is Rob Otis right to be concerned?**

Will robots replace teachers?

Will we say 'goodbye' to our favourite teachers soon and 'hello' to robot teachers? Some people think this will happen by 2027. The problem is, there just are not enough teachers!

Robots have taken many jobs over the years. Planes can now use autopilot and you can shop online with no need for a shop assistant. The big question schools are now asking is 'Will robots replace teachers?'

Some schools have already started using artificial intelligence (AI) in the classroom. The AI teacher, otherwise known as the mechanical teacher, is exactly as it sounds. It's a computer that is programmed to teach and test children. It matches work to their needs and has already had great results.

5 📖 **Read and respond.**

    a 👥 ✏️ Read the next part of the article on the worksheet. Find evidence that the writer does *not* believe that robots will replace teachers.

    b 👥 💬 Do you think Rob Otis agrees with the magazine article?

6 📖 **Read an interview with the director of a robotics company in Finland. Their robot is already being used to teach language in schools.**

> **Why do you think the new language teacher robot iLangbot should be used in schools?**
>
> The robot keeps children active and engaged. It can be designed to match a curriculum and a well-programmed robot does not make mistakes.
>
> **Why do you think they should replace teachers?**
>
> With a robot, children can practise language without fear of making mistakes. It is neutral. It does not laugh if you make mistakes. Unlike a teacher, it does not get tired of repeating words or answering questions.

    a 👥 💬 What is the director's point of view on robots?

    b 🧑 ✏️ Write three reasons that the director gives for why robots should be used. Use the worksheet.

    c 👥 💬 Would you like to learn a language with a robot?

Talking point

Has your opinion about robots replacing teachers changed? Explain your thoughts using information you have looked at today.

Before you go

Make a list of the advantages and disadvantages of robots in the classroom.

5.6 Facing challenges

✓ Evaluation
✓ Analysis
✓ Reflection

1 What do you think of this rule?

> NO MOBILE PHONES IN THE CLASSROOM.

2 What are the advantages and disadvantages of having mobile phones in schools?

3 Why do you think schools should use technology?

> Don't you think it would be amazing if we learned how to make computer games?

> I think it could be helpful if I want to be an engineer when I am older.

4 Read and respond.

> My teacher says he **doesn't believe computers help us learn or think** better.

> That could be because **teachers find them difficult**. They might **need lessons** too!

> I've heard they're just **confused** about what to buy. **Everything changes so fast**.

> Yes, it must be **very expensive** to invest in new things all the time.

> Maybe, they should ask an expert …

> Can they be trusted? **Sellers could be biased**. They might just want to sell you one of their products.

> Well, I know my teacher is really **worried about** our **safety**.

> There are **internet filters** at school, but they can be **frustrating**. We can't get onto most websites.

> Schools are also **worried** that children will have **health problems**. They say we will get **eye strain** and we need to **exercise** more.

a Explain the challenges of using technology in the classroom in your own words.

b Make a note of the challenges of using technology in the classroom in the table on the worksheet.

5 **Read and respond.**

> Using computers and tablets in schools is so much **fun**!

> It's great when we get to **join in** with quizzes and play **interactive** games.

> We **feel like we are playing** games, **but** then we realise we are **learning**.

> Yes, and you **know straight away** if you have made a **mistake** and you **get to try again**.

> I enjoy **controlling my learning**. I can **organise my tasks** and I can **see my progress**.

> You can **find answers** to your questions **quickly** online.

> And you can **share information easily**. You send stuff electronically or print things out.

> My teacher says we will need these **skills** in our **future jobs**.

> It's not bad for **teachers** too! It can make their **life easier**. They can give us **work** they find online and get **ideas** to use in class.

a Explain the benefits of using technology in the classroom in your own words.

b Note the benefits of using technology in the classroom in the table on the worksheet.

6 **Look at your completed table on the worksheet. Are there any points you agree or disagree with?**

Talking point

What skills did you use to help you to identify the different perspectives?

Before you go

Why do you think schools might decide not to use the latest technology?

5.7 How is technology used?

1 👥 💬 How did you use technology when you were little?
How has the way you use it changed now that you are older?

2 👥 💬 Look at the pictures. How many of these activities have you done?

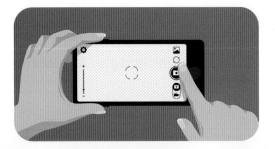

3 👥 💬 Read this request from a head teacher. Help him find a research question.

> I want to invest in some new technology. To help me decide what our school needs, I would like to know what children are using.

4 Plan the investigation.

a 👥 📖 Look at the planning table on the worksheet. Talk about what you need to do in your groups.

b 👥 ✏️ Plan your investigation using the table on the worksheet.

Designing a questionnaire

- Decide what you want to find out.
- Give details of the investigation.
- Write questions to suit the purpose of the investigation.
- Check that questions are suitable and well-written.
  - ✓ The question looks at a single problem.
  - ✓ It is easy to answer.
  - ✓ The answer is short – tick, one word, yes/no.
  - ✓ The question is easy to understand.
  - ✓ The answer helps to understand the problem.
- Test the questionnaire in a small group.

5 **Organise your team.**

a Read the job descriptions carefully and choose roles that suit your skills.

Leader
Keeping to time
Making sure everyone knows what to do and has a job
Giving and explaining ideas

Challenger
Thinking what might go wrong
Checking questions
Explaining ideas to the leader

Scribe
Writing and reading what the group decides
Helping to explain and report ideas

Helper
Looking out for who needs help
Telling the leader who you have decided to help

b What questions will you write? Share some good questions and check if they will give you the answers you need.

Which of these do you use most in class? ✓
Tell me about the last time you used a computer in class. ✗ **Answer too long!**
Which of these do you prefer to use? ✓
Do you like using computers or do you prefer to use tablets? ✗ **More than one question!**

c Work as a team to write your questions. Use the worksheet.

6 **Now try out your questionnaire.**

a Test your questions on other teams to check that they give the answers you expect.

b Make changes to your questions if you need to.

Talking point

Did you enjoy your role today? Why, or why not?

Before you go

Can you guess what the results of your investigation will be?

5.8 Technology questionnaire

1 👥 💬 **Look at questionnaires A and B. Who are they both aimed at?**

A

What do you like most about school?			
Books	🙂	😐	🙁
Food	🙂	😐	🙁
Friends	🙂	😐	🙁
Outside play	🙂	😐	🙁

B

What do you like most about school?					
Statement (Tick to show how you feel about each statement.)	Strongly Disagree	Disagree	Neutral	Agree	Strongly agree
My teachers help me at school.					
I know what I need to do to improve.					
I like learning new things.					
I like coming to school.					
I enjoy spending time with friends at school.					

2 👥 💬 **Who is your questionnaire for? Review your plan from the last lesson and discuss how you could organise your questionnaire.**

3 👥 💬 **Look carefully at these questions. Which style do you prefer? Why?**

- How are the responses recorded?
- Do they use pictures or words?
- Which do you think are the easiest to use?
- Which do you think are the easiest to understand?

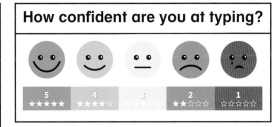

How often do you do research using a computer?				
Never	a little	sometimes	often	very often

Which do you use?	
	tablet
	computer
	camera
	smart phone
	sound recorder

How confident are you at typing?

4 👥 **Plan the layout of your questionnaire.**

a 👥 💬 Decide how you will organise your team to complete the task.

b 👥 ✏️ Complete the design of your questionnaire. Use the checklist.

5 👥 💬 **Conduct your investigation.**

a 👥 💬 Ask your questions and collect responses.

b 👥 💬 Evaluate your questionnaire. Use these questions to help you.

- Were people able to answer your questions easily?
- Were you happy with the order of your questions?
- Are your results clear?
- How could you improve your questionnaire?

6 👥 💬 **Present your questionnaires as a team. Explain your choices and give an evaluation of your questionnaire.**

Checklist

Questionnaire checklist

✓ Are your questions simple and clear?

✓ What is the best order for your questions?

✓ How will responses be recorded?

Talking point

How does your questionnaire provide answers to the research question?

Before you go

Do you think you would make a good researcher?

Unit 5 Final task:
Investigate and report on the future of technology in schools

Read the final task and discuss the question.

> Work in **teams** to investigate the **opinions** of **adults** and **children** on the **future of technology** in **school**. **Collect** and **analyse data**, using questions provided by a local tech company. **Present** a **report** to show your findings, explaining the **different perspectives**. Conclude your report with a **personal reflection** explaining any **changes** in your **own opinions**.

1 **What do you need to do to be successful in this task? Use the words in bold to help you.**

2 **A tech company wants your help. They would like to know the opinions of adults and children in your school. It will help them to design technology for the future. Read the questions to find out what they want to know.**

- Do you think technology will improve the way we learn in the future?
- Is more technology in the classroom a good thing?
- Do you think we should reduce technology in schools in the future?
- What do you think we will use technology for most in the next 10 years?
- What concerns do you have about using more technology in schools?
- What is the main advantage of using technology in schools?
- Should we use technology in schools?
- Do you feel confident when trying new technology?
- What would you like our company to invent for the future?

a How good are the company's questions? Use the tips for writing survey questions in Lesson 5.7 to help you.

b Choose the best three questions for your survey.

3 **Organise your team. Choose roles to suit your skills and decide how you will organise yourselves to collect information for your survey.**

Leader	
• Keeping to time	
• Making sure everyone knows what to do and has a job	
• Giving and explaining ideas	

Challenger
• Thinking what might go wrong
• Checking questions
• Explaining ideas to the leader

Scribe
• Writing and reading what the group decides
• Helping to explain and report ideas

Helper
• Looking out for who needs help
• Telling the leader who you have decided to help

4 **Plan and complete your survey.**

a Plan your investigation to find out the opinions of children and adults in your school about the future of technology. Use these questions to help you.

• What is the purpose of the investigation?

• What do you want to find out?

• How will you collect your data?

• Who will you ask?

• How many people will you ask?

• What opinions will you be asking about? *Use your chosen questions to help you answer this.*

b Write your questionnaire. Remember to consider how you will record your responses.

c Carry out your survey.

5 **Review how different charts and graphs can be used to show your results.**

a Use ideas from previous lessons to help you decide how you will show your results.

b Organise your results so you can compare opinions easily.

c What opinions did children and adults have about the future of technology in schools? Use the results of your survey to discuss what you discovered and how their opinions compare.

6 **Organise your team to write a report to present to the tech company.**

a Write a report to explain your findings to the tech company.

b Present your team reports and share your opinions on the results.

Reflection: How successful was our investigation and report?

a 👤✏️ Complete the final task checklist. Use the worksheet.

b 👥💬 Share your checklist with your team. Do you all agree?

Final task checklist			
Our questionnaire gives answers to the research question.	🙂	😐	🙁
The results are clear and easy to analyse.	🙂	😐	🙁
Our report includes the main points of different opinions.	🙂	😐	🙁
The report is clear and well organised.	🙂	😐	🙁
We included comments to explain personal opinions.	🙂	😐	🙁

c 👥💬 Take turns to say what you did to help the team. Do you all agree?

d 👤✏️ Reflect on your personal perspective. Answer the questions on the worksheet.

Before you go

👥💬 Discuss these questions in pairs.

What did you enjoy most about this task?

What did you find most difficult about this task?

How well did you work as a team?

How did your team help you during the task?

What have you learned in this unit?

Glossary

bias: a strongly held opinion that is influenced by experiences; people can show bias when they believe something is one way, even if it is not accurate

closed question: a question where the person is asked to choose from one of several given answers; this makes information quicker to collect and the limited choice makes responses easier to analyse

collaborate: when two or more people work together on a task

evacuate: to send someone away from a dangerous place to somewhere safe

fact: something that can be proved to be true

infographic: a text with pictures, numbers and symbols to help us understand information about a topic

investigation: the process of collecting, analysing and interpreting data

log: a record of all details and events relating to a particular thing

market research: collecting information to help a company sell their products or services – who buys them and what they want

open question: a question where the person asked can give any answer they want; open questions often ask for reasons, explanations and descriptions

opinion: a thought or belief about something, which cannot be proved to be true or false

perspective: a viewpoint on an issue based on evidence and reasoning.

predict: to think what will happen in the future

primary source: information that comes directly from someone involved in the event being researched; it is original information that can be fact or opinion

product research: research to find out if a new product or service might be successful and how best to sell it

questionnaire: a set of questions created to find out what people think about a topic

relevant: important or significant to a particular situation or person

researcher: someone who collects, organises, analyses and interprets data and opinions to explore issues, solve problems and predict

research question: the main question you use to find information during research on a topic

secondary source: a report, summary or interpretation of information from a primary source; it does not give original information

source: the place where you have found information during research; include the title, author and date

survey: a way to find out information from a lot of different people by asking them all the same question

unbiased: fair; not affected by someone's opinions

Acknowledgements

The publishers wish to thank the following for permission to reproduce photographs. Every effort has been made to trace copyright holders and to obtain their permission for the use of copyright materials. The publishers will gladly receive any information enabling them to rectify any error or omission at the first opportunity.

Cover and title page Visuals Stock / Alamy Stock Photo, p.1 B Calkins/Shutterstock, p.2 ymgerman/Shutterstock, p.2 Colorfuel Studio/Shutterstock, p.3 SewCream/Shutterstock, p.6 Andriy Blokhin/Shutterstock, p.6 Smileus/Shutterstock, p.6 moxumbic/Shutterstock, p.6 homeworlds/Shutterstock, p.6 wessam Noufal/Shutterstock, p.6 NTL studio/ Shutterstock, p.7 Andrey Armyagov/Shutterstock, p.7 ImageFlow/Shutterstock, p.8 EB Adventure Photography/Shutterstock, p.8 Roman Samborskyi/Shutterstock, p.9 BalkansCat/Shutterstock, p.10 Pressmaster/Shutterstock, p.11 Riccardo Mayer/Shutterstock, p.11 Paramarta Bari/Shutterstock, p.12 Vladimir Turkenich/Shutterstock, p.12 sculler/Shutterstock, p.12 COULANGES/Shutterstock, p.14 Text © Catriona Clarke 2017, Illustration © HarperCollins Publishers 2017, p.14 Text © Catriona Clarke 2017, Illustration © HarperCollins Publishers 2017, p.15 Text © Catriona Clarke 2017, Illustration © HarperCollins Publishers 2017, p.16 invens/Shutterstock, p.16 Oil and Gas Photographer/Shutterstock, p.17 WowAnna/Shutterstock, p.18 Tsetsen Ubushiev/Shutterstock, p.18 Anton Petrus/Shutterstock, p.18 elly_kei/Shutterstock, p.18 nadia_if/Shutterstock, p.19 iQoncept/Shutterstock, p.21 Evgeny Atamanenko/Shutterstock, p.22 Nicoleta Ionescu/Shutterstock, p.23 Brocreative/Shutterstock, p.24 Mikushina_a_happy/Shutterstock, p.24 LightField Studios/Shutterstock, p.24 Dean Drobot/Shutterstock, p.24 Prostock-studio/Shutterstock, p.24 Atstock Productions/Shutterstock, p.24 LightField Studios/Shutterstock, p.24 anueing/Shutterstock, p.25 Ben Gingell/Shutterstock, p.26 mypokcik/Shutterstock, p.26 Ground Picture/Shutterstock, p.28 matimix/Shutterstock, p.28 Kornn/Shutterstock, p.30 Marish/Shutterstock, p.31 AnnaStills/Shutterstock, p.32 aleksandr_pa_vector/Shutterstock, p.32 Mostovyi Sergii Igorevich/Shutterstock, p.32 Wojmac/Shutterstock, p.32 Gilang Prihardono/Shutterstock, p.32 Paisit Teeraphatsakool/Shutterstock, p.33 80's Child/Shutterstock, p.33 Reshetnikov_art/Shutterstock, p.35 Rawpixel.com/Shutterstock, p.36 dieddin/Shutterstock, p.36 lev radin/Shutterstock, p.38 Iuliia Skalskaia/Shutterstock, p.38 NaMong Productions/Shutterstock, p.39 KK Tan/Shutterstock, p.41 joerngebhardt68/Shutterstock, p.42 Zurijeta/Shutterstock, p.42 thka/Shutterstock, p.42 Kingmaya Studio/Shutterstock, p.43 PlutusART/Shutterstock, p.44 Naty.M/Shutterstock, p.44 tomeqs/Shutterstock, p.44 VectorArtist7/Shutterstock, p.44 Electric Egg/Shutterstock, p.44 BW Folsom/Shutterstock, p.44 Dionisvera/Shutterstock, p.46 Thinglass/Shutterstock, p.46 mentatdgt/Shutterstock, p.47 TommyStockProject/Shutterstock, p.47 New Africa/Shutterstcok, p.47 Pixel-Shot/Shutterstock, p.47 max dallocco/Shutterstock, p.48 Jane Kelly/Shutterstock, p.48 Orange Vectors/Shutterstock, p.48 Flat.Icon/Shutterstock, p.48 Creative Stall/Shutterstock, p.48 ElkhatiebVector/Shutterstock, p.48 Banana Walking/Shutterstock, p.48 M-O Vector/Shutterstock, p.48 SharafMaksumov/Shutterstock, p.50 LadadikArt/Shutterstock, p.50 MisterEmil/Shutterstock, p.50 Andrey_Popov/Shutterstock, p.52 Canteen: Five Stars/Shutterstock, p.52 davooda/Shutterstock, p.55 GraphicsRF.com/Shutterstcok, p.55 StockSmartStart/Shutterstock, p.55 StockSmartStart/Shutterstock, p.55 VectorStudio CanD/Shutterstock, p.55 StockSmartStart/Shutterstock, p.55 Voinau Pavel/Shutterstock, p.55 SpeedKingz/Shutterstock, p.55 SpeedKingz/Shutterstock, p.55 SpeedKingz/Shutterstock, p.58 Stokkete/Shutterstock, p.61 astarot/Shutterstock, p.62 conzorb/Shutterstock, p.62 Africa Studio/Shutterstock, p.62 Sabina Leopa/Shutterstock, p.62 Real_life_photo/Shutterstock, p.62 MidoSemsem/Shutterstock, p.63 4Max/Shutterstock, p.64 AsiaTravel/Shutterstock, p.64 tynyuk/Shutterstock, p.64 olmazik/Shutterstock, p.64 GoodStudio/Shutterstock, p.64 A. Bizgaimer/Shutterstock, p.65 Tavarius/Shutterstock, p.65 AnnGaysorn/Shutterstock , p.65 Pavel L Photo and Video/Shutterstock, p.65 vectorica/Shutterstock, p.65 Aleutie/Shutterstock, p.66 AlexStreln/Shutterstock, p.66 Shyamalamuralinath/Shutterstock, p.67 M-Production/Shutterstock, p.67 tanitost/Shutterstock, p.67 maxart/Shutterstock, p.68 Monkey Business Images/Shutterstock, p.68 Monkey Business Images/Shutterstock , p.68 fa5/Shutterstock, p.68 ARLOU_ANDREI/Shutterstock, p.68 Zoran Zeremski/Shuttersock, p.68 DONOT6_STUDIO/Shutterstock, p.68 Jacob Lund/Shutterstock, p.68 Vectorbum/Shutterstock, p.68 LightField Studios/Shutterstock, p.70 gorillaimages/Shutterstock, p.70 pong-photo9/Shutterstock, p.70 Gorodenkoff/Shutterstock, p.70 RoBird/Shutterstock, p.70 K.Ladjimi/Shutterstock, p.71 Dmytro Zinkevych/Shutterstock, p.73 Lemberg Vector studio/Shutterstock, p.74 Stephen Coburn/Shutterstock, p.76 wavebreakmedia/Shutterstock, p.76 NYS/Shutterstock, p.78 Federico Rostagno/Shutterstock, p.81 Ground Picture/Shutterstock, p.82 Monkey Business Images/Shutterstock, p.82 Pixel-Shot / Shutterstock, p.82 Rido/Shutterstock, p.82 George Rudy/Shutterstock, p.82 LeManna/Shutterstock, p.84 dpa picture alliance archive / Alamy Stock Photo, p.86 Gorodenkoff/Shutterstock, p.86 Illust_monster/Shutterstock, p.86 Pixel-Shot/Shutterstock, p.86 wavebreakmedia/Shutterstock, p.86 New Africa/Shutterstock, p.86 goodluz/Shutterstock, p.87 Gorodenkoff/Shutterstock, p.88 MemoriesStocker/Shutterstock, p.88 Marius Dobilas/Shutterstock, p.88 Ammit Jack/Shutterstock, p.88 wavebreakmedia/Shutterstock, p.88 akramalrasny/Shutterstock, p.88 Apisorn/Shutterstock, p.90 yamasan0708/Shutterstock, p.91 Phonlamai Photo/Shutterstock, p.92 Veja/Shutterstock, p.94 pizzastereo/Shutterstock, p.94 Tartila/Shutterstock, p.94 Macrovector/Shutterstock, p.94 Wise ant/Shutterstock, p.94 YummyBuum/Shutterstock, p.94 RedlineVector/Shutterstock, p.94 Iconic Bestiary/Shutterstock, p.94 Anatolir/Shutterstock, p.94 Net Vector/Shutterstock, p.95 Alena Nv/Shutterstock, p.96 Oleon17/Shutterstock, p.96 ivector/Shutterstock, p.96 Rawpixel.com/Shutterstock, p.96 Zyn Chakrapong/Shutterstock, p.97 bioraven/Shutterstock, p.98 Gorodenkoff/Shutterstock.

Definitions adapted from Collins Cobuild Dictionary.